STEWARDSHIP

Karyn Henley

Standard
PUBLISHING

CINCINNATI, OHIO

STEWARDSHIP

The foundation for reflecting God

Karyn Henley

FOUNDATIONS CURRICULUM

Published by Standard Publishing, Cincinnati, Ohio
A division of Standex International Corporation

Credits
Cover design by Brian Fowler
Interior design by Jeff Richardson
Cover and inside illustrations by Ed Koehler
Project editors: Ruth Frederick, Bruce E. Stoker

08 07 06 05 04 03 02   5 4 3 2 1
ISBN 0-7847-1368-5
Printed in the United States of America

TABLE OF CONTENTS

Introduction
Introduction
Introduction

INTRODUCTION

The Irish poet William Butler Yeats once said, "Education is not the filling of a pail, but the lighting of a fire." In the first temple, the tent of meeting, there was a lampstand. God's instructions were, "Tell the people of Israel to bring you pure olive oil for the lampstand, so it can be kept burning continually. . . . Aaron and his sons will keep the lamps burning in the Lord's presence day and night" (Exodus 27:20, 21, NLT). Today we are God's temple (1 Corinthians 3:16). And our passion, our living love for the Lord, keeps our lampstand burning before him. (See Revelation 2:4, 5.) Our job in the spiritual education of children is to light a fire, a living, growing love for God within them.

The Foundations curriculum can help light that fire. Each of our students is a temple of God. So the goal of the Foundations curriculum is to construct within children the essential foundations upon which they can build (and sustain) a loving, thriving relationship with the Lord. To do this, the Foundations curriculum provides a thorough, step-by-step, in-depth exploration of the following foundations.

Quarter 1: Studying the Bible, The Foundation for Knowing God

Quarter 2: Salvation, The Foundation for Living with God

Quarter 3: Prayer, The Foundation for Growing Closer to God

Quarter 4: Worship, The Foundation for Loving God

Quarter 5: Lordship, The Foundation for Following God

Quarter 6: Stewardship, The Foundation for Reflecting God

Quarter 7: Missions, The Foundation for Sharing God

Quarter 8: Making Peace, The Foundation for Living in Fellowship

This curriculum is intended for use with students in third through fifth grades. Each quarter is independent of the others, so they can be taught in any order. In fact, each quarter can be used as a single unit to fill in a 13-week study at any time of the year and can be followed or preceded by any other curriculum of your choice.

The following arrangement is a suggestion showing how the Foundations Curriculum can be taught in two years. Studying the Bible (September-November), Salvation (December-February), Prayer (March-May), Worship (June-August), Lordship (September-November), Stewardship (December-February), Missions (March-May), Making Peace (June-August).

WALK THROUGH A WEEK

SCRIPTURE AND GOAL

The session begins with a Scripture and a simple goal. You may use the Scripture as a memory verse if you wish, or you may use it to support the theme for the day, reading the Scripture when you gather for the first prayer.

INTRODUCTORY ACTIVITY

You can begin your introductory activity as soon as the first student arrives, guiding others to join you as they come into your room. This activity serves two purposes. First, it gives the students something fun to do from the first moment they arrive. Second, it starts thoughts and conversations about the theme of the session. Talking is encouraged. Questions are welcome. Get to know your students. Make it your goal to discover something interesting and special about each one. Let them know that their mission is to discover more about God and about how they can get to know him better every day, so that God becomes their constant companion, their treasured friend, their awesome king.

DISCOVERY RALLY

Gather the students together as a group in preparation for the Discovery centers.

What's the Good Word? This is a time to read the Scripture for the day. You may also sing a few songs if you want.

Challenge. This is a time to introduce the students to the theme for the day by making challenging statements or asking challenging questions.

Prayer. Choose a student to lead a prayer of blessing for the day's activities, asking God to open your hearts and teach everyone present.

DISCOVERY CENTERS

You will need either one teacher/facilitator for each center, or clearly written instructions that tell the students what they are to do in the center.

The way your class uses Discovery Centers will depend on how much time you have and how many students there are in your class.

• If you have a few students, go together to as many centers as you can in the time you have.

• If you have more than ten students and lots of time, divide into three groups. Send one group to each center and let each group rotate to a different center as they finish the activity, so that each student gets to go to each center during Discovery Center time.

• If you have more than ten students, but little time, divide into groups of three. Number off, one to three in each group. Each student #1 goes to the first center, #2 goes to the second, #3 goes to the third. After each center has completed its activity, the original groups of three come back together again to tell each other what they learned in their centers.

• Or you may choose to let all three centers do the same activity. Choose the one or two activities that you think your students will enjoy most. Divide the students into groups for centers, and once they are there, do not rotate. Instead, let each group do the one or two activities you have chosen.

DEBRIEFING QUESTIONS

If you have time, gather together as a large group at the end of the session to ask and answer questions and discuss the theme and/or other issues on the students' minds.

Review the Scripture for the day.

PRAY

You or a student may close your class time in prayer.

SERVICE OPPORTUNITIES

If you don't have service opportunities for your class to be involved in, here are some that you can check into. You may want to simply tell your class about these groups, you may want to give financially to these groups, or you may want to join these groups in a hands-on project.

BIBLE MISSION INTERNATIONAL

Helps people in the former Soviet Union. Offers child sponsorships for needy children.
P.O. Box 484
Wichita, KS 67201-0484
(877) 264-4247
www.biblemission.org

BOOK OF HOPE

Offers opportunity to help support the distribution of Bibles around the world for $1 per Bible given away.
3111 SW 10th St.
Pompano, FL 33069
(800) 448-2425
www.bookofhope.org

COMPASSION INTERNATIONAL

Offers sponsorship for needy children around the world.
P.O. Box 7000
Colorado Springs, CO 80933-9849
(800) 336-7676
www.compassion.com

HABITAT FOR HUMANITY

Builds affordable housing around the world for those who would not otherwise be able to own a house.
121 Habitat St.
Americus, GA 31709-3498
(800) HABITAT
www.habitat.org

HEIFER PROJECT

Offers group projects to provide the purchase of animals for the poor around the world. Also available: a hunger awareness/action program.
P.O. Box 8058
Little Rock, AR 72203
(800) 422-0474
www.heifer.org

SAMARITAN'S PURSE/OPERATION CHRISTMAS CHILD

Collects gifts packed in shoe boxes for needy children around the world. Franklin Graham is the Chairman of this organization.
801 Bamboo Road
P.O. Box 3000
Boone, NC 28607
(800) 353-5949
www.samaritanspurse.org

WORLD CONCERN

Offers hands-on opportunities for children to get involved through global gifts and share kits.
19303 Fremont Ave. N.
Seattle, WA 98133
(800) 755-5022
www.worldconcern.org

> **Note:** The author and publisher do not endorse any of these organizations in preference to any other organization that helps the needy. This is simply a partial list of opportunities available to you. If you should decide that you are interested in one of them, it is your responsibility to explore these opportunities and prayerfully decide whether and to what extent you should be involved in them.

What Is a Steward?

Scripture

"For we are God's masterpiece. He has created us anew in Christ Jesus, so that we can do the good things he planned for us long ago." Ephesians 2:10, NLT

Goal

Learn that a steward is a manager and has responsibilities.

INTRODUCTION

Place several kinds of snacks on paper plates, one type of snack per plate. Pour juice into paper cups and set them on a table. When the first student arrives, ask her to be the juice steward. She is to offer the other students some juice as they arrive. As the other students enter, give each one a plate of snacks, telling them to circulate around the room, offering each person some of the snacks on their plate. The students can serve each other and eat.

DISCOVERY RALLY

Discovery Rally
y Rally

Gather the students together in a large group.

WHAT'S THE GOOD WORD?

Choose a student to read the Scripture for the day.

THE CHALLENGE

Ask: **According to the Scripture we just heard, what did God create us for?**
Point out that in the introductory activity, they were serving each other. Say:
The good things we do serve each other and God. God has created us to be "stewards." A steward is a manager for someone who is in authority. In our case, God is in authority over us, and we are managers over all he has given us.

Tell the students that in the next few weeks, they will discover more about the things over which God has made us managers. In their Discovery Centers today they will find out what a steward is.

PRAYER

DISCOVERY CENTERS

Discovery Centers
y Centers

1. BIBLE STEWARDS

DO: Play this game like "Go Fish." If you have more than four students, make two groups. Each group will need 36 cards, two of each kind. Mix the cards up and deal three to each student. The remaining cards go into the "Steward Pile," facedown in the center of the group. To begin, one student asks another, "Do you have _____?" naming a particular card in his own hand. If the other student has the card, he gives it to the first student who then has a pair. He places that pair on the table and may ask another student for another card. If the other student did not have the match-

> **MATERIALS**
> for every four students, you'll need two copies of each of the Bible Stewards pages (pages 13, 14), with the cards cut out (36 cards), Bibles

ing card, that student says, "Look again." Then the first student draws the top card from the "Steward Pile." If it's a match, he may put the pair on the table, but may not ask for another card. Play moves to the student on his left who now becomes the one who asks someone else for a card. Students try to be the first to match all their cards.

DISCUSS: After a round or two of play, say: **Let's find out more about some of these stewards.** Ask someone to read Genesis 39:1-4 to find out about Joseph. Ask someone to read Genesis 43:16, 17, 24 to find out what Joseph's steward did. Ask someone to read 1 Kings 18:3 to find out about Ahab's steward. Ask: **What kind of person makes a good steward?**

2. STATIONERY

DO: Give each student four sheets of paper and envelopes. Ask the students to write across each bottom border: "I am a letter from Christ. 2 Corinthians 3:3." Then they may design the borders

for their stationery with the markers, crayons, rulers, and stickers. If they have time, they may design the backs of their envelopes to match.

DISCUSS: Ask someone to read 2 Corinthians 3:2, 3. Ask: **What does it mean to be a letter from Christ? Who reads us?** Review the Scripture for the day. Ask: **What does it mean to be a masterpiece? What were we created for?** Say: **Doing good things is a way that we can be stewards of God. We are stewards of all God has given us. As we do good with what he has given us, we are seen and "read" like a letter God sends to the world, telling about himself.**

3. UNIFORMS FOR THE LORD'S STEWARDS

DO: Give each student a copy of the Uniforms page. Ask students to use the code to fill in the blanks and find out what the uniform is for the Lord's stewards.

MATERIALS
copies of the Uniforms for the Lord's Stewards (page 15), pencils, a Bible

DISCUSS: Say: **A steward is a manager for someone who is in authority. In our case, God is in authority over us, and we are managers over all he has given us.** Ask someone to read Ephesians 6:14-17. Ask how each of these items would help a steward of God. Ask: **What kind of person makes a good steward?**

DISCOVERERS' DEBRIEFING

If you have time to review, gather as a large group and discuss your young discoverers' findings. Ask the following questions:

• **What is the most interesting thing you discovered today?**
• **What did you learn today that you did not know before?**
• **What is a steward?**
• **What kind of person makes a good steward?**
• **What does it mean to be a letter from Christ? Who reads us?**
• **What were we created for?**

Review the Scripture for today.

Pray, thanking God for creating us to be his masterpieces and his letters to the world. Ask him to help us be good stewards of all he has given us.

NOTE: Before you send the students home, make sure each has a copy of the reproducible note to parents on the following page. It is essential that this note go home in preparation for next week's session.

FROM YOUR CHILD'S TEACHER

Dear Parent,

As you may know, we are involved in a series of lessons concerning stewardship. It is our goal to help each student understand what a steward is, and to understand that God intends for us to be good stewards over all he has given us.

We are planning a project next week that will help children understand that we are to be stewards over the earth, the plants, and the animals that God created. For that we need your help. We are asking that each student bring an empty, clean 2-liter soda bottle from home.

It is a pleasure to be able to teach your child about stewardship. Thank you for helping us accomplish that task. Feel free to call with any questions.

Teacher_____

Phone_____

Bible Stewards

Joseph's Steward

Ziba
Steward of Saul's Grandson

King Xerxes' Steward

Cuza
Manager of Herod's Household

Joseph
Steward at Potiphar's House

Obadiah
In Charge of Ahab's Palace

Azmaveth
In Charge of David's Storehouse

Ezri
In Charge of David's
Farm Workers

Shimei
In Charge of David's Vineyards

Baal-Hanan
In Charge of David's
Olive and Sycamore Trees

Joash
In Charge of David's
Olive Oil Supplies

Shaphat
In Charge of David's
Herds in the Valley

Obil
In Charge of David's Camels

Jehdeiah
In Charge of David's Donkeys

Jaziz
In Charge of David's Sheep

The Ethiopian
In Charge of the Queen's
Treasuries

Kenaniah
In Charge of David's Singers

Benaiah
In Charge of David's Bodyguard

Uniforms for the Lord's Stewards

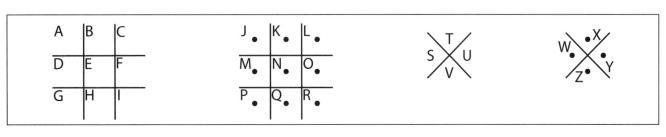

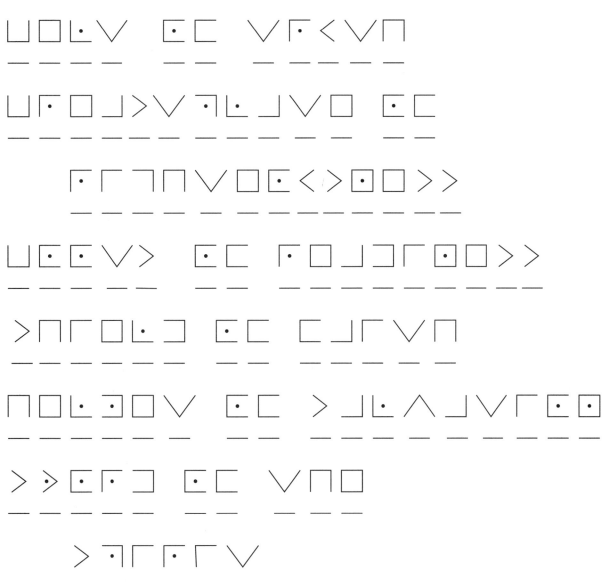

Stewards of the Earth

scripture

"Then God said, 'Let us make people in our image, to be like ourselves. They will be masters over all life....'"
Genesis 1:26, NLT

Goal

Learn that God created us to be stewards over the earth.

INTRODUCTION

Bring magazines that have nature scenes in them. When students arrive, collect the empty soda bottles that they bring. These will be used in Discovery Center #1. Then give each student a piece of construction paper. Ask students to cut nature scenes out of the magazines and glue them onto construction paper to make a montage. Ask them to tell about their favorite thing in nature or a favorite place they've gone to experience God's natural world.

DISCOVERY RALLY

Gather the students together in a large group.

WHAT'S THE GOOD WORD?

Choose a student to read the Scripture for the day.

THE CHALLENGE

Ask: **What did God mean when he said that people were to be "masters over all life"?** Say: **God did not make us owners of his creation. He made us managers or stewards of his creation.** Ask: **What's the difference between an owner and a manager? If we own creation, we can do whatever we want with it for our own purposes. If we manage creation, we do what God wants with it, for his purposes.** Say: **God intended for us to be good managers of his creation.**

Tell the students that in their Discovery Centers today they will find out more about being stewards of the earth.

PRAYER

DISCOVERY CENTERS

1. BIRD FEEDERS

DO: Give each student a soda bottle. Ask each student to draw two large windows on the sides of the soda bottle as shown below. Then you punch a hole with an ice pick or sharp knife in one of the corners of each window. This will give the students a place to insert their scissors and cut out the windows. Also punch a hole in the neck of the bottle through one side and out the other. Give each student a 20" piece of string to thread through the holes in the neck of the bottle. Students tie the ends of the string together. Now students use the hole punch

MATERIALS

For each student you'll need one empty, clean 2-liter soda bottle. (Bring a few extras in case someone forgets.) You'll also need one straight drinking straw or chopstick per student, permanent markers, string, scissors, hole punchers, an ice pick or sharp knife for teacher's use, a Bible

to punch two holes in opposite sides of the bottom section of the bottle as shown below, one hole beneath each window. They stick the straw or chopstick through one hole and out the other. Students may draw designs on this bird feeder with permanent markers.

DISCUSS: As the students work, ask: **What is a steward? How can we be good stewards of the earth? How can we be good stewards of the animals God created? How will this bird feeder help you be a good steward of God's creation? You will feed the birds, and you will recycle a plastic bottle. What is an "endangered" animal? How do people help endangered animals? How is that being a good steward of God's creation?** Ask someone to read Proverbs 12:10. Ask: **Do you have pets? If so, what kind? How can you be a good steward of your pets?**

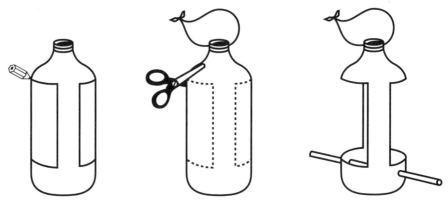

2. EMBOSSED LEAVES

MATERIALS

a variety of leaves (from trees, bushes, and vegetables), aluminum foil, construction paper, scissors, stapler and staples, glue, markers, a Bible

DO: Give each student two pieces of construction paper. They fold one piece in half and cut out a large rectangle, starting at the fold. This becomes a border when opened. Set the leaves in a pile, and tell students to choose two leaves each. These they arrange face down on their first piece of construction paper. Give each student a piece of aluminum foil the size of the construction paper. They place this on top of the leaves. Now they rub over the foil with their fingers, revealing the leaf shapes lying beneath. Then remove the leaves and staple the aluminum foil to the construction paper. Glue the border on top, and write across the lower border: "'God gives plants of the field to everyone.' Zechariah 10:1."

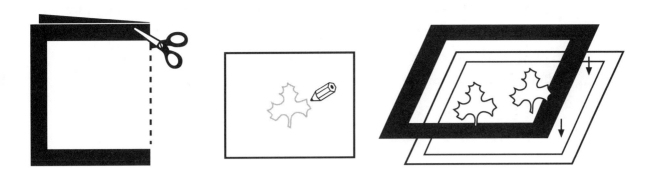

DISCUSS: Ask someone to read Zechariah 10:1. Ask someone else to read Psalm 24:1, 2. Ask someone to read Deuteronomy 10:14. Ask: **Who does the earth belong to? Why? How can we be stewards of God's earth? Why do people cut down trees? How are they being good stewards when they plant trees to take the place of those they cut down? How can you be a good steward of your own yard or neighborhood?**

3. A MEADOW IN A POT

MATERIALS
small plastic or terra cotta pots, disposable picnic bowls, packing "peanuts," potting soil, plastic spoons, ryegrass seed or bird seed, water, a Bible

DO: Give each student a pot and bowl. Ask students to set the pots into the bowls. Then they put a few packing peanuts into the pot to keep soil from slipping out of the hole in the bottom. They add potting soil until it's about 1/2" from the rim of the pot. They should sprinkle bird seed over this and then cover the seed with about 1/4" of soil. Students should water the newly planted seed so that the soil is damp, but not soaked. Tell the students to take these home and place the pots in a place where they'll get light. They should water the seeds lightly each day to keep the ground moist, but not soaked. In a few days, their potted meadows should start sprouting.

DISCUSS: Ask someone to read Psalm 104. Ask: **Do people own the earth? What does Psalm 104 tell us about the One who owns the earth? What does it tell us about grass and plants?** Say: **God has made us stewards over the earth. What is a steward? What does it mean to be a steward of God's creation? What are some practical ways that you can be a steward of the earth? Besides taking care of plants and animals, here are some other**

suggestions: Reduce what you waste by not buying things you don't need, by using less stuff, by recycling everything you can. Save energy by turning off lights when you leave a room. Save water by turning the water off while you brush your teeth. You save three gallons of water per brushing this way!

DISCOVERERS' DEBRIEFING

If you have time to review, gather as a large group and discuss your young discoverers' findings. Ask the following questions:

- **What is the most interesting thing you discovered today?**
- **What did you learn today that you did not know before?**
- **What did God mean when he said that people were to be "masters over all life"?**
- **Do people own the earth?**
- **What is a steward?**
- **What does it mean to be a steward of God's creation?**
- **What are some practical ways that you can be a good steward of the earth?**

Review the Scripture for today.

Pray, thanking God for his creation. Tell the Lord that we know the earth is his and we are simply stewards of it. Ask God to help us be good stewards of his creation.

Stewards of Time

Scripture

"There is a time for everything, a season for every activity under heaven." *Ecclesiastes 3:1, NLT*

Goal

Learn that God made us managers of time, and we are responsible for using time wisely.
Learn that either we let God control our time, or our time controls us.

INTRODUCTION

As students arrive, teach them to play "Around the Clock." Divide the students into groups with at least three in each group, but not more than six. Each student will need a button. Each group will need a pair of dice and a copy of the clock page from the end of this session plan. Players roll the dice and count the dots to see who goes first: the one with the highest number is first. The first player rolls the dice, hoping to get a 1 and start the journey around the clock. If he gets a 1, he places his button in the 1 space. The player to his left takes a turn. If the first player does not get a 1, he has to wait for his turn to come back around so he can try for a 1 again. Continue with everyone working their way around the clock. For numbers above 1, players can count both dice. And if the needed number turns up on one die, and the second die shows the following number (example: 3 and 4), the player can advance to space three and space four. Otherwise, as long as the dots showing equal the number they need, players can move to the next space. The one who reaches 12 first wins.

DISCOVERY RALLY

Gather the students together in a large group.

WHAT'S THE GOOD WORD?

Choose a student to read the Scripture for the day.

THE CHALLENGE

Say: **It's great to have all of you time travelers with us today.** Check your watch to see how long it has been since class began. Tell everyone that they've traveled that many minutes in time. Ask them to think back to last night when they went to bed, then think of when they woke up this morning. Say: **You travel about eight hours through time every night. Even when you are completely still, you are traveling through time. We travel through time at the speed of 24 hours per day.** Ask someone to read Genesis 1:14. Ask: **Who created time? Do we own time?** Say: **We are stewards or managers of time. If we let God control our time, he will give us all the time we need. If we don't let God control our time, our time controls us. Have you known people who are hurried and worried and controlled by their schedules?**

Tell the students that in their Discovery Centers today they will find out more about managing the time that God has given us.

PRAYER

DISCOVERY CENTERS

1. TIMELY WISDOM

MATERIALS
a copy of the Time-Wise Beginnings and Time-Wise Endings (pages 27, 28), scissors, a Bible

DO: Before class, cut apart the beginnings and endings. Mix up the beginnings. Mix up the endings. Give each student one beginning and one ending. One student reads her beginning and ending. The other students say whether this beginning and ending go together or not. If they don't, the student who thinks he has the correct ending reads it. Students can look up the reference in the Bible to find out whether it is correct or not.

DISCUSS: Ask: **What did you learn from these Proverbs about managing time? What are some good things to do with time? What are some wasteful things to do with time?** Say: **If we dedicate our time to God (becoming God's steward), he makes sure we have plenty of time. If we don't let God control our time, our time controls us. We become time's slave.** Ask: **What do you think it's like to be a slave to time?**

2. WHO'S IN CONTROL POSTERS

MATERIALS
disposable picnic plates with divided compartments and no designs on them, permanent fine-point markers or ball point pens, one piece of white poster board for each student, glue

DO: Students will start these posters this week and complete them next week. You should make one of these posters as well and post it in the room. Give each student a plate. Ask them to turn the plate so the two small panels are at the top and the large panel is at the bottom. Ask students to use markers or ball point pens to write on the borders of the plate. On the upper right border, they write in small letters, "Psalm 86:11." On the upper left border, they write, "Colossians 3:23." On the lower left border, they write, "Matthew 6:33, 34." On the lower right border, they write, "Proverbs 3:5, 6." Direct them to write "GOD" in the center of the plate, "1. Keep Praying" in the upper right panel, "2. Seek God first. 3. Don't worry: trust." in the large lower panel, and "4. Do what God gives you." in the upper left panel. Now give each student a piece of poster board. Ask the students to picture this poster board as the dashboard and windshield of a car. They should glue the plate on as if it were the steering wheel. Tell them they will finish this poster next week.

DISCUSS: Say: **We've said that either we let God control our time, or our time controls us. This plate represents a steering wheel and tells us how to put God in control. What is number 1?** Ask someone to read Psalm 86:11. Explain that this is a prayer that King David prayed. Ask: **What could we pray in order to put God in control of our time? We can pray like David did.** Suggest also praying, "Lord, be the Keeper of my Time and the Order of my life." Ask: **What is the second thing to do to let God control?** Ask someone to read Matthew 6:33, 34. Ask: **How can we seek God first with our time? What is the third thing to do to let God control?** Ask someone to read Proverbs 3:5, 6. Ask: **How can we trust God with our time and not worry about it? What is the fourth thing to do?** Ask someone to read Colossians 3:23. Say: **We do what God give us to do with our time. This is a cycle that we do over and over again as we let God control everything we're stewards over.**

3. A NECK PILLOW

MATERIALS
handkerchiefs or bandanas (or 21" square fabric pieces), fabric ribbon, polyester fiberfill stuffing, fabric markers, a Bible

DO: Give each student a handkerchief or bandana and two to three handfuls of fiberfill. They place the fiberfill along one edge of the bandana and roll the bandana as if making a tube with the fiberfill inside. Then students tie the ends of the bandana with fabric ribbon as shown. If you have used handkerchiefs or fabric with no design on it, students may want to draw designs on these pillows with fabric markers.

DISCUSS: Ask someone to read Exodus 20:8-11. Ask: **What does "holy" mean? It means set apart, different, special. What makes the seventh day different? It's a day of rest. There is a time to work and a time to rest. Some people think that resting is a waste of time.** Ask someone to read Psalm 46:10. Ask: **What came before "knowing God" in this verse? Being still came first.** Ask someone to read Luke 10:38-42. Ask: **What did Martha choose to do with her time? What did Mary choose to do with her time? What did Jesus say?** Say: Sometimes we're so busy that we skip the most important thing: being with God. There is a time just to rest and be with God. Either we let God control our time, or our time controls us.

DISCOVERERS' DEBRIEFING

If you have time to review, gather as a large group and discuss your young discoverers' findings. Ask the following questions:

- **What is the most interesting thing you discovered today?**
- **What did you learn today that you did not know before?**
- **What does the book of Proverbs say about managing time?**
- **What are some good things to do with time?**
- **What are some wasteful things to do with time?**
- **What are four things to do to put God in control of our time?**
- **Why is it important to be good managers or stewards of time?**
- **What makes the seventh day different?**
- **Explain what happens if we don't allow God to control our time.**

Review the Scripture for today.

Pray, thanking God for giving us the gift of time. Ask him to help us to be good stewards and managers of our time.

Around the Clock

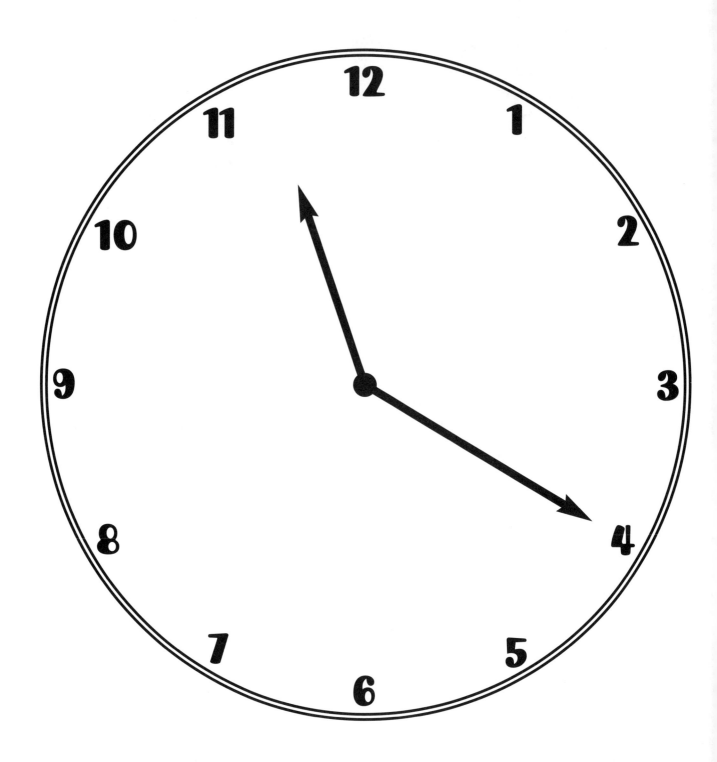

Time-Wise Beginnings

"Don't brag about tomorrow since..." Proverbs 27:1	"A person who moves too quickly may..." Proverbs 19:2
"Don't weary yourself trying to get rich. Why waste your time? For..." Proverbs 23:4, 5	"Hard work means prosperity;..." Proverbs 12:11
"A little extra sleep, a little more slumber, a little folding of the hands to rest and..." Proverbs 24:33, 34	"Ants—they aren't strong, but..." Proverbs 30:25
"God has made everything beautiful for..." Ecclesiastes 3:11	"God has planted eternity in the human heart, but even so..." Ecclesiastes 3:11
"A wise youth works hard all summer... Proverbs 10:5	"Finishing is better than starting. Patience is better than..." Ecclesiastes 7:8
"If you wait for perfect conditions,..." Ecclesiastes 11:4	"It's wonderful to be young!..." Ecclesiastes 11:9

Time-Wise Endings

"...you don't know what the day will bring."	"...go the wrong way."
"...riches can disappear as though they had the wings of a bird!"	"...only fools idle away their time."
"...poverty will pounce on you like a bandit."	"... they store up food for the winter."
"...its own time."	"...people cannot see the whole scope of God's work from beginning to end."
"...a youth who sleeps away the hour of opportunity brings shame."	"...pride."
"...you will never get anything done."	"Enjoy every minute of it."

Stewards of Money and Possessions

Scripture

"Honor the Lord with your wealth." Proverbs 3:9, NLT

Goal

Learn that God made us managers of money and possessions, and we are responsible for using them wisely.
Learn that either we let God control our money and possessions or our money and possessions control us.

INTRODUCTION

Before class, gather a variety of items of large and funny clothing and accessories: hats, ties, gloves, shoes, aprons, glasses, etc. Place them in a large shopping bag. Also bring an audiotape player and a tape of music. As students arrive, ask them to form a circle. When you start the music, they begin passing the bag around the circle. Stop the music at random. Whoever holds the bag, reaches into the bag without looking and pulls out an item. This student must put this item on over his or her own clothes. Then you start the music, and the bag goes around the circle again. Students who arrive later join the game at a time when you stop the music. (You may want to bring your camera for a group photograph after the game.)

DISCOVERY RALLY

Gather the students together in a large group.

WHAT'S THE GOOD WORD?

Choose a student to read the Scripture for the day.

THE CHALLENGE

Ask: **What is wealth? Wealth is having more than we need to survive. How many of you have a car or van? How many of you have a pantry or refrigerator that has food in it right now? How many of you have more than one bedroom in your house?** Say: **Many people in the world don't have even one car, much less two. Many people in the world don't have enough food for the rest of the day. So those of us gathered here are all wealthy people. God expects us to be good stewards of our wealth. We can choose to dedicate our wealth to God, or try to keep it for ourselves. But we must remember that either we let God control our money and possessions, or our money and possessions control us.** Tell the students that in their Discovery Centers today they will find out more about how to be good stewards or managers with their money and possessions.

PRAYER

DISCOVERY CENTERS

1. WHO'S IN CONTROL POSTER

DO: Give the students the posters they began making last week. Ask them to draw the windshield and dashboard around their steering wheel.
Ask them to write across the top of the poster: "Let God Drive." Remember to complete your poster and display it in the room. You will use it next week.

MATERIALS
markers and crayons, the posters that students started last week

DISCUSS: Say: **We've said that either we let God control our money and**

possessions, or let our possessions control us. Ask: **What does this poster tell us to do to put God in control? What could we say in prayer about our possessions? How can we seek God first with our money and possessions? How do we trust him with our possessions? Then we do what God wants us to do with our money and possessions.** Tell the students that this is a cycle that we do over and over again as we let God control everything we're stewards over.

2. WEALTH WISDOM

DO: Before class, cut apart the beginnings and endings. Mix up the beginnings. Mix up the endings. Give each student one beginning and one ending. One student reads her beginning and ending. The other students say whether this beginning and ending go together or not. If they don't, the student who thinks he has the correct ending reads it. Students can look up the reference in the Bible to find out whether it is correct or not.

DISCUSS: Ask: **What did you learn from Proverbs about managing wealth and possessions? What are some good things to do with possessions? What are some wasteful things to do?** Say: **If we dedicate our possessions to God, he makes sure we have all we need. Either we let God control our possessions, or our possessions control us. We become their slave.** Ask: **What do you think it's like to be a slave to possessions?**

3. WHEN WE GIVE

DO: Give each student a pencil and a copy of the When We Give page. Tell the students to take the first letter off of each word and put it onto the end of the word before it. The first letter of the first word goes onto the end of the last word. Then ask them to read the decoded verse aloud together.

DISCUSS: Ask: **What does this verse mean? What can we give besides money?** Ask someone to read Matthew 6:19, 20. Ask: **How can we store up treasures in heaven?** Ask students to give specific suggestions. Ask someone to read Luke 12:15-21. Ask: **How can we be rich toward God? If life isn't measured by how much we own, what is life measured by?** Ask someone to read Ecclesiastes 5:19. Ask: **What kinds of wealth and possessions has God given most of the people you know? Do you own your possessions, or does God? Do you own your money, or does God? God owns everything. We are simply stewards and managers of what he has given us. We are responsible to use it wisely.** Say: **Either we let God control our wealth and possessions, or our wealth and possessions control us.**

DISCOVERERS' DEBRIEFING

If you have time to review, gather as a large group and discuss your young discoverers' findings. Ask the following questions:

• **What is the most interesting thing you discovered today?**
• **What did you learn today that you did not know before?**
• **Do you own your money and possessions, or does God? Explain.**
• **What are four things to do in order to put God in control of our money and possessions?**
• **How can we be good stewards of our wealth and possessions?**
• **What did you learn from Proverbs about managing possessions?**
• **What are some good things to do with wealth and possessions? What are some wasteful things to do with wealth and possessions?**
• **How can we store up treasures in heaven?**
• **Explain what happens if we don't allow God to control our possessions.**

Review the Scripture for today.

Pray, thanking God for the wealth and possessions he has given us. Ask him to help us be good stewards and managers of our wealth and possessions.

Wealth-Wise Beginnings

"Wealth from get-rich-quick schemes…" Proverbs 13:11	"Wealth from hard work…" Proverbs 13:11
"It is better to have little with fear for the Lord than to…" Proverbs 15:16	"Trust in your money and… Proverbs 11:28
"The rich and the poor have this in common: The Lord…" Proverbs 22:2	"Don't weary yourself trying to get rich. Why waste your time? For riches…" Proverbs 23:4, 5
"It is better to be poor and honest than…" Proverbs 28:6	"The person who wants to get rich quick…" Proverbs 28:20
"Those who are stingy…" Proverbs 11:24	"Tell those who are rich in this world not to be proud and not to…" 1 Timothy 6:17
"People who long to be rich…" 1 Timothy 6:9	"For the love of money…" 1 Timothy 6:10

Wealth-Wise Endings

"...quickly disappears."	"...grows."
"...have great treasure with turmoil."	"...down you go!"
"...made them both."	"...can disappear as though they had the wings of a bird!"
"...rich and crooked."	"...will only get into trouble."
"...will lose everything."	"...trust in their money, which will soon be gone."
"...fall into temptation and are trapped by many foolish and harmful desires."	"...is at the root of all kinds of evil."

When We Give

"PGIV   EAN   DI   TWIL   LB   EGIVE

_____   _____   _____   _____   _____   _____

NT   OYO   UGOO   DMEASUR   EPRESSE

_____   _____   _____   _____   _____

DDOW   NSHAKE   NTOGETHE   RAN

_____   _____   _____   _____

DRUNNIN   GOVE   RWIL   LB   EPOURE

_____   _____   _____   ____   _____

DINT   OYOU   RLA."   Luke 6:38

_____   _____   _____

Stewards of Talents

Scripture

"To those who use well what they are given, even more will be given, and they will have an abundance".
Matthew 25:29, NLT

Goal

Learn that God made us managers of our talents, and we are responsible for using them wisely.
Learn that either God controls our talents, or our talents (or lack of talents) control us.

INTRODUCTION

As students arrive, give each of them an unsharpened pencil and a kneadable eraser. Ask students to mold their eraser onto the top of the pencil in the shape of something that represents a talent or skill they have, or something they are interested in, or something they'd like to do well someday. For example, a student who is talented in piano may mold his eraser into the shape of a piano, or a musical note. A student who is talented at baseball may mold her eraser into the shape of a baseball. As students finish, ask them to show their erasers and let others guess what their talent is.

DISCOVERY RALLY

Gather the students together in a large group.

WHAT'S THE GOOD WORD?

Choose a student to read the Scripture for the day.

THE CHALLENGE

Review the past few weeks. Ask: **What is a steward's job? It's to manage something for someone who's an owner or person in authority.** Ask students to tell you what they've been given as stewards or managers for God. Say: **You've all been given something else that is uniquely your own. The person sitting next to you probably has a different one. Can you guess what it is? It is your talents. There are certain things that you can do well. Not all people can do what you can do.** Refer back to today's Scripture. Say: **If we dedicate our talents to God, he will make sure we have all the talents that we need. If we don't dedicate our talents to God, either our talents will control us, or we'll be forever searching for our hidden talents and abilities.** Refer to the Who's in Control poster on display on the wall. Remind students of the four things to do to put God in control of our talents: (1) keep praying that God will control your talents; (2) seek God first before your talents; (3) don't worry about your talents; trust God with them; (4) do with your talents what God gives you to do. Tell the students that in their Discovery Centers today, they will find out more about how to be good stewards and managers of their talents.

PRAYER

DISCOVERY CENTERS

1. WHAT'S MY TALENT?

DO: Give each student a pencil and piece of paper. Ask students to think of a talent they have or would like to have someday. Ask them to think of someone they admire

MATERIALS
pencils and paper

and might want to be like someday. Or ask them to think of a place they'd like to work someday. If they still can't think of anything, whisper something that you think they'd be good at. Then they write a description of that talent, skill, or job without naming it. Then each student takes a turn reading his description, and the others guess what talent it describes.

DISCUSS: Say: **God has given us a way to know what our talents are: joy. Usually when we enjoy doing something, we are talented at it. That's one thing school is good for. It helps us try different things to find out what talents God has given us. It's just as important to find out what we dislike as it is to find out what we like.** Ask: **How can you glorify God with the talents you have?** (Thank him for the talents he's given you. Become excellent in using your talents. Use them to help and bless others. Help others to become excellent too.) Say: **Either we let God control our talents, or our talents control us. If we don't trust God with showing us our talents, we may not even find our talents. What would it be like to have talents control you? What would it be like never to know your real talents?**

2. MILLIONS OF TALENTED PEOPLE

DO: Give each student a pencil and piece of paper. Ask students to use the yellow pages to find and list the jobs that start with the first letter of their name. Let each student read the list they collected.

MATERIALS
paper, pencils with erasers, and several copies of your phone book's "yellow pages" index

DISCUSS: If students have written any businesses that do not glorify God, ask them to erase the business. Explain that the people in these businesses will never have the full joy and satisfaction that God intends for people to have in their talents. Use this opportunity to discuss the fact that God allows people to choose to use their talents for his Kingdom. Say: **God gives talents to everyone in the world, even to people who don't know or thank him. However, either we let God control our talents, or our talents control us. If we're not trusting God, we may never even find our talents.** Ask: **How can we be good stewards of our talents? How can we put God in control of our talents? How can we put God before our talents? How can we trust God with our talents?**

3. PROFILES

DO: Give each student a piece of paper and a marker. Divide the group into pairs. One student lays her head sideways on the paper while her partner traces around her profile. Then they trade places. Now ask the students to write seven different intelligence types in the border around the profile: (1) Word Smart, (2) Numbers Smart, (3) Pattern Smart, (4) Music Smart, (5) Sports Smart, (6) People Smart, (7) Self Smart.

MATERIALS

large pieces of construction paper, non-permanent markers, a Bible

DISCUSS: Tell students that learning researchers have found everyone is "smart" in some way. Some people are smart in more that one of these ways. Ask students to circle the areas in which they think they are smart. Then ask: **How can you find out what your talents are?** Say, **First, pray and ask God to show you. Second, ask people who know you well. Third, try different things to find out what you enjoy. Never believe someone who tells you that you are not smart or that you can't do anything right. God gives everyone talents.** Ask someone to read Psalm 138:8. Ask: **How can we be good stewards of our talents? What four things we can do to let God control our talents?**

DISCOVERERS' DEBRIEFING

If you have time to review, gather as a large group and discuss your young discoverers' findings. Ask the following questions:

- **What is the most interesting thing you discovered today?**
- **What did you learn today that you did not know before?**
- **How can you find out what your talents are?**
- **How can you glorify God with the talents you have?**
- **What happens if we don't let God control our talents?**
- **What are four things we can do to put God in control of our talents?**

Review the Scripture for today. Pray, thanking God for giving us talents. Ask God to help us be good stewards and managers of our talents.

Stewards of Relationships

scripture

"A friend is always loyal, and a brother is born to help in time of need." Proverbs 17:17, NLT

Goal

Learn that God made us managers of relationships, and we are responsible for treating others respectfully.
Learn that either we allow God to control our relationships, or our relationships control us.

INTRODUCTION

As students arrive, give each one a copy of Scrambled Fruit (page 44). Ask them to unscramble the fruits of the Spirit on the vine. For help, they may look up Galatians 5:22, 23.

DISCOVERY RALLY

Gather the students together in a large group.

WHAT'S THE GOOD WORD?

Choose a student to read the Scripture for the day.

THE CHALLENGE

Ask students to list the fruits that they unscrambled. Ask if they see a connection between those fruits and the Scripture for the day. Say: **When Jesus is our Lord, his Holy Spirit lives within us. And when his Holy Spirit lives within us, these fruits grow and show in our lives, and our friendships and family relationships grow stronger.** Ask: **Does a loving person make a good friend and family member? Does a joyful person make a good friend and family member? How about a peaceful person? A patient person? A kind person? A good person? A gentle person? A faithful or loyal person? A self-controlled person?** Say: **God expects us to be good stewards of our relationships. Either we allow God to control our relationships, or our relationships control us.** Refer to the Who's in Control poster. Ask: **What four things can we do to put God in control of our relationships?** Tell the students that in their Discovery Centers today they will find out how to be good stewards or managers of their relationships.

PRAYER

DISCOVERY CENTERS

1. THE MISSING FRUIT

DO: Before class wash the grapes and strawberries. These will be eaten. If you want to eat any of the other fruits, bring a knife to slice them. Place one of each type of fruit on the tray. Give the students 30 seconds to look at the fruit. Then take the tray away and remove one fruit. Bring the tray back and ask them to raise their hand when they discover which fruit is missing. Hold up each fruit and ask which fruit of the Spirit starts with the same first letter. Ask them to clean their hands and let them snack.

MATERIALS

a tray or large flat box, a lime, a package of fruit gelatin, a pineapple, a pear, kiwi fruit, grapes, figs, grapefruit or guava, strawberries, plastic spoons and disposable picnic bowls, paper towels, hand cleansing gel or wipes

DISCUSS: Ask: **Why do you think God gives us relationships? To be good**

stewards of relationships, we must do things God's way. **What is God's way of making relationships work?** Remind them of the fruits of the Spirit. Say: **Either we allow God to control our relationships, or our relationships control us. What would it be like to have our relationships control us?** (We make friends or family more important to us than God. We worry about who likes us. We don't allow the fruits of the Spirit to influence our relationships. We fuss and argue. Ask: **Can we put God in control of our relationships? How can we seek God first before our relationships? How can we trust God with our relationships?** Say: **We do what God gives us to do in the relationships he gives us.**

2. A HAND WREATH

MATERIALS
large pieces of construction paper, tape, pencils, scissors, markers

DO: Give each student a different color of construction paper, a pencil, and scissors. Ask students to trace as many of their own handprints as they can get on the paper. Then they cut out the handprints. Now students trade some of their handprints so that they each have a variety of colors. Each student arranges his handprints in a circle with the hands overlapping a bit. Use small loops of tape to secure the overlapping parts. Put strips of tape over the back sides of the hands to secure them. On the top hand, they write "God." Then on the other hands, they write the names of people with whom they have relationships.

DISCUSS: Ask: **How can you be a good steward of a relationship with a friend? How can you be a good steward of family relationships? How can you allow God to control these relationships? What kinds of friends will help you honor God? What might make relationships difficult? How can the fruits of God's Spirit help make relationships better?**

3. PEOPLE WISDOM

MATERIALS
a copy of People-Wise Beginnings and People-Wise Endings (pages 45, 46), a Bible

DO: Before class, copy and cut out the beginnings and endings. Mix the beginnings up. Mix the endings up. Then give each student a beginning and an ending. Let students take turns reading their beginnings and endings. The other students try to decide if they go together. If not, they decide who has the ending that matches. Look up the Scripture to find out if they're correct.

DISCUSS: Ask: **What did you discover from these proverbs about managing relationships? Why does God give us relationships? Why does he want us to be good stewards of our relationships? How can these proverbs help us in our relationships?** Say: **Either we let God control our relationships, or our relationships control us. How can a relationship control us?** (We make friends or family more important to us than God. We worry about who likes us and who doesn't. We don't allow the fruits of the Spirit to have an influence on our relationships. So we fuss and argue. We allow our disappointment and frustration with people to control our moods.)

DISCOVERERS' DEBRIEFING

If you have time to review, gather as a large group and discuss your young discoverers' findings. Ask the following questions:
- **What is the most interesting thing you discovered today?**
- **What did you learn today that you did not know before?**
- **What is a relationship? Why does God gives us relationships?**
- **How can we be good stewards or managers of relationships?**
- **How can you allow God to control these relationships?**
- **How can the fruits of God's Spirit help make relationships better?**
- **What did you discover from Proverbs about managing relationships?**
- **What happens when we don't let God control our relationships?**
- **What are four things we can do to put God in control of our relationships?**

Review the Scripture for today. Pray, thanking God for giving us relationships, especially with family and friends. Ask God to help us be good stewards and managers of our relationships.

Scrambled Fruit

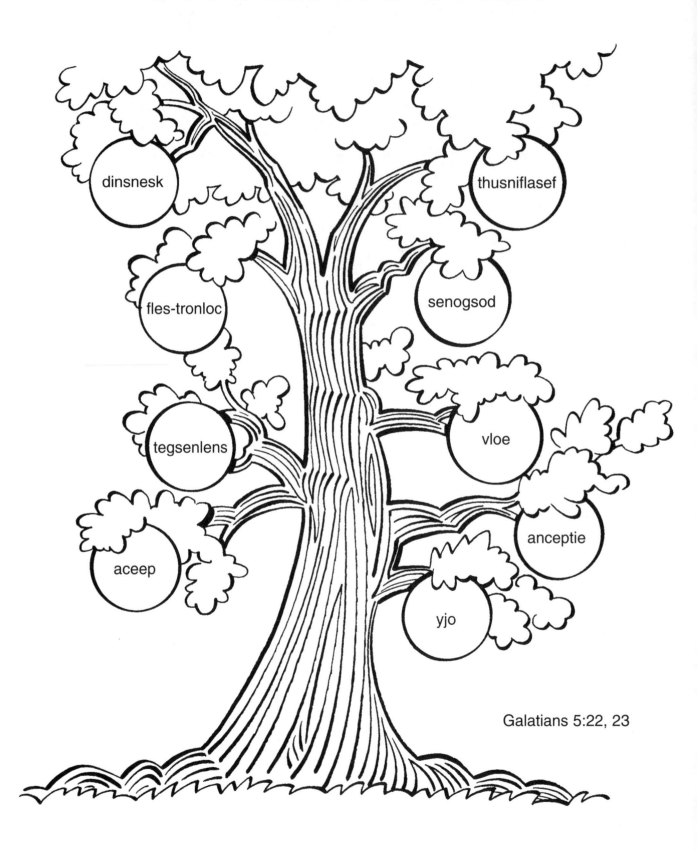

dinsnesk

thusniflasef

fles-tronloc

senogsod

tegsenlens

vloe

anceptie

aceep

yjo

Galatians 5:22, 23

People-Wise Beginnings

"Faithful messengers are as refreshing as…" Proverbs 25:13	"A person who doesn't give a promised gift is like…" Proverbs 25:14
"Those who bring trouble on their families inherit…" Proverbs 11:29	"Don't visit your neighbors too often or you will wear out your…" Proverbs 25:17
"Someone who lies to a friend and then says, 'I was only joking is like…" Proverbs 26:18, 19	"Only a fool despises a parent's discipline; whoever learns from correction is…" Proverbs 15:5
"Kind words are like…" Proverbs 16:24	"A dry crust eaten in peace is better than…" Proverbs 17:1
"The heartfelt counsel of a friend is as sweet as…" Proverbs 27:9	"Arguments separate friends like…" Proverbs 18:19
"A nagging wife annoys like…" Proverbs 19:13	"Children who mistreat their father are…" Proverbs 19:26

People-Wise Endings

"...snow in the heat of summer. They revive the spirit of their employer."	"...clouds and wind that don't bring rain."
"...only the wind."	"...welcome."
"...a mad man shooting a lethal weapon."	"...wise."
"...honey—sweet to the soul and healthy for the body."	"...a great feast with strife."
"...perfume and incense."	"...a gate locked with iron bars."
"...a constant dripping."	"...a public disgrace and an embarrassment."

God Equips His Stewards to Speak

Scripture

"We all have different gifts. Each gift came because of the grace that God gave us. If one has the gift of prophecy, he should use that gift with the faith he has. If one has the gift of serving, he should serve. If one has the gift of teaching, he should teach. If one has the gift of encouraging others, he should encourage. If one has the gift of giving to others, he should give freely. If one has the gift of being a leader, he should try hard when he leads. If one has the gift of showing kindness to others, that person should do so with joy."   Romans 12:6-8, ICB

Goal

Learn that God has given some of his stewards "speaking" gifts.

INTRODUCTION

Set out crayons. As students arrive, give each one a copy of Good and Perfect Gifts (page 53). Ask students to color in the spaces in which the numbers add up to ten. They will find the word that completes the James 1:17 Scripture.

DISCOVERY RALLY

Gather the students together in a large group.

WHAT'S THE GOOD WORD?

Choose a student to read the Scripture for the day.

THE CHALLENGE

Ask your students if any of them have ever read, heard, or seen a video of *The Lion, the Witch, and the Wardrobe* by C. S. Lewis. Describe the special gifts Father Christmas gave to three of the children in the story. Say: **Aslan gave a shield and sword to Peter, a bow and arrows and a small ivory horn to Susan, and a dagger and small bottle of healing liquid to Lucy.** Ask: **Why did Father Christmas give them gifts? He knew they would need these gifts to help others as they went on their journey.** Say: **Life on earth is like a journey. God has a purpose for every person. But he doesn't want to send us through life by ourselves. God wants to help us. He wants us to invite him to go along with us to guide us on our journey. And he gives each person gifts to use to help others.** Remind them of the gifts that the Scripture mentioned: teaching, prophecy, encouraging, serving, leading, giving, and kindness. Say: **God has given each of you one or more of these gifts to help you be a good steward and manager.**

Tell the students that some of these gifts are "speaking" gifts, and some are "doing" gifts. Tell them that in their Discovery Centers today, they will learn about the "speaking" gifts.

PRAYER

DISCOVERY CENTERS

1. CONCENTRATION

MATERIALS
four copies of Concentration (page 54) with the cards cut out, two Bibles

DO: Divide your students into two groups. Each group will need two of each different Concentration card. In each group, turn all cards face down and mix them up. Line them up in several rows. Choose one student to go first. This student chooses two cards and turns them face up. If they match, she keeps the cards, looks up the Scripture listed on the cards, and reads it. Then she turns two more cards over. As long as she gets matches, she continues her turn. If the two she turns over do not match, she turns them face down again, and the student on her left takes a turn trying to find a match. Continue the play until all cards have been matched.

DISCUSS: Ask students to list some of the Bible people who were teachers. Say: **Teachers learn and then tell what they've learned to others.** Ask students to list some encouragers. Say: **Encouragers help others to have courage and hope. They cheer others up and help them see that they have value in God's Kingdom.** Ask the students to name some prophets. Say: **A prophet is someone who knows God's ways. He sees clearly what's right and wrong, and says so.** Ask if any of them think they might be teachers, encouragers, or prophets. Point out that Jesus was all of these. Ask: **How do these gifts help us become good stewards and managers?**

2. POT AND POTTER

MATERIALS
play dough, a rolling pin, wax paper, plastic knives, toothpicks, a Bible

NOTE: If you want to make the play dough, mix 1 part salt, 1 part water, and 4 parts flour. Add more water as needed to make the dough workable but not sticky.

DO: Give each student a large piece of wax paper for their work surface. Then give them some play dough. Ask them to roll out the dough or pat it flat with their hands until they have a rectangle of dough about 1/4" thick. With plastic knives, they cut the dough in half lengthwise. Then they cut the dough in half width-wise. Now they have four rectangles of dough. They cut only one of the quarters in half width-wise. One of the remaining three rectangles becomes the bottom of their "slab pot." Students stand the other two long rectangles up along the length of the bottom of the pot and pinch the bottom edges together. These become the long sides of the pot. The remaining small pieces of dough are the short ends of the pot. Students stand them up and pinch the sides and bottoms of the pot together as shown. Students use the toothpicks to write their initials or names at one end of their pot. These will be left with you so that they may finish them next week. You may leave them out to air dry, or bake them at 350 degrees for 30 to 45 minutes.

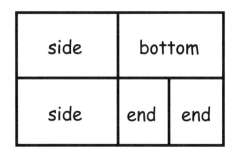
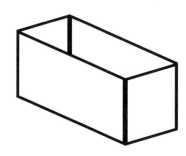

You may want to make a few more slab pots for possible visitors next week, or for students who were absent this week.

DISCUSS: As the students work, read Isaiah 45:9-12. Ask: **What is God saying in this Scripture? What are some different kinds of things that a potter can make out of clay?** Say: **Each of us is like a different piece of pottery. Each of us has a purpose and a gift to help fulfill that purpose. Some of us have speaking gifts: teaching, encouraging, and prophecy. What do teachers do?** Teachers learn and then tell what they've learned to others. **Teachers don't have to be in a classroom. Teachers can be in other jobs. Still, they enjoy telling others what they know. What do encouragers do? They help others to have courage and hope. They cheer people up and help them see that they have value in God's Kingdom. What do prophets do?** Explain that this doesn't necessarily describe people like the Old Testament prophets. Say: **A prophet is someone who knows God's ways. He sees clearly what's right and wrong, and says so.** Ask the students if any of them think they have the gift of teaching, or encouraging, or prophecy. If they don't know, tell them that's all right. Now that they know about these gifts, they can start noticing their natural tendencies and be aware that God will develop at least one of these gifts within them. Ask: **Why does God give these gifts to us? It's one of the ways that God prepares us to be good stewards and managers.**

3. FOLD AND DRAW

MATERIALS
paper, crayons or non-permanent markers

DO: Give each student a piece of paper. Ask students to fold their paper into three fairly equal sections and then unfold the paper. Ask them to imagine a face drawn on this page. In the top section only, they are to draw the top of the hair, the eyebrows (but not eyes), and the forehead. On the top left hand side of this section, they write the word "prophet." On the top right hand side, they write "see and tell God's will." Now they fold the top section back so that it is hidden, and they pass the paper to the student on their left.

Now students draw on the middle section. Tell them to draw eyes, ears, and nose in this section. To the left, they write, "teacher." To the right, they write, "learn and teach God's truth." Then they fold this second section back so that it is hidden, and they pass the paper to the student on their left.

Now students draw on the bottom section. Tell them to draw the mouth, chin, and neck. To the left, they write, "encourager." To the right, they write, "cheer and bring God's hope." Then they pass the paper to the student on their left.

Now students unfold their papers and show everyone the faces they've drawn. They will leave these with you and complete them next week.

DISCUSS: Ask someone to read Psalm 139:14. Then ask the students to think of how they were made. Ask if any of them think they might have the gift of teaching or encouraging or prophecy. Assure them that if they don't know what their gift is, they can now be aware of these different gifts and watch for their gift to emerge in their lives. Their gift will be something that comes natural to them. Ask: **Why does God give us these gifts? It's one of the ways that God prepares us to be good stewards and managers.**

DISCOVERERS' DEBRIEFING

If you have time to review, gather as a large group and discuss your young discoverers' findings. Ask the following questions:

- **What is the most interesting thing you discovered today?**
- **What did you learn today that you did not know before?**
- **How are we like something that a potter would create?**
- **What are the "speaking" gifts that God gives?**
- **What does a teacher do? What does a prophet do? What does an encourager do?**
- **Why does God give us these gifts?**

Review the Scripture for today.

Pray, thanking God for giving us these gifts. Ask God to show each of us what our gifts are and to help us use these gifts to become good stewards and managers for him.

Good and Perfect Gifts

Fill in the spaces that add up to 10 to find the word that completes the verse:

"Every good and perfect gift is from _____." James 1:17

Concentration

Encourager  **Hezekiah** 2 Chronicles 32:1-8	**Encourager**  **Jesus** Matthew 14:27	**Encourager**  **Barnabas** Acts 11:22, 23
Teacher  **Solomon** 1 Kings 4:33, 34	**Teacher**  **Apollos** Acts 18:24, 25	**Teacher**  **Jesus** Matthew 7:28, 29
Prophet  **Jesus** Matthew 21:11	**Prophet**  **John the Baptist** Matthew 11:7-10	**Prophet**  **Samuel** 1 Samuel 3:19-21

God Equips His Stewards to Do

Scripture

"We all have different gifts. Each gift came because of the grace that God gave us. If one has the gift of prophecy, he should use that gift with the faith he has. If one has the gift of serving, he should serve. If one has the gift of teaching, he should teach. If one has the gift of encouraging others, he should encourage. If one has the gift of giving to others, he should give freely. If one has the gift of being a leader, he should try hard when he leads. If one has the gift of showing kindness to others, that person should do so with joy." Romans 12:6-8, ICB

Goal

Learn that God has given some of his stewards "doing" gifts.

INTRODUCTION

As the students arrive, give each one the slab pot he made last week. If you have visitors or students who were absent last week, and you did not make pots for them, give them play dough to make their pots at this time. Have acrylic paints, paintbrushes, cups of water, paper towels, and newspaper available. Cover the work surface with newspaper. Give each student a small paper plate. Students place on their plates a dollop of each color of paint they want. Then they design and paint their slab pots. Remind the students of Isaiah 45:9-12 which they read last week.

DISCOVERY RALLY

Gather the students together in a large group.

WHAT'S THE GOOD WORD?

Choose a student to read the Scripture for the day.

THE CHALLENGE

Before class, place two large disposable plastic cups on a tray or large shallow box lid. In one cup, place a handful of pens or pencils. In the other cup, place several pairs of blunt scissors. Also place a stack of index cards on the tray. As you gather in a large group, set the tray somewhere near you. After the Scripture is read, say: **Last week we talked about....** As you talk, reach for the tray, but do it quickly, and intentionally tip the tray as you bring it in front of you so that all the contents of the tray spill off in the floor. Don't ask anyone to help you clean it up. Instead, begin picking it up yourself and see who helps you. When you've cleaned up the mess, ask:

- **Who helped me without being asked? They probably have the gift of serving.**
- **Who wanted to tell others what to do to help me? They probably have the gift of leadership.**
- **Who would have given me your own pencil to use if I had lost mine? They probably have the gift of giving.**
- **Who wanted to say, "That's okay. Everybody spills things sometime"? They probably have the gift of kindness.**
- **Who wanted to say, "You should have been more careful"? They probably have the gift of prophecy.**
- **Who wanted to say, "The things on the tray spilled because they weren't balanced properly"? They probably have the gift of teaching.**
- **Who wanted to say, "Cheer up. You're still a good teacher. A few spilled pencils won't hurt anything"? They probably have the gift of encouraging.**

Remind the students that last week they learned about the "speaking" gifts: teaching, prophecy, and encouragement. Tell them that in their Discovery Centers today they will learn about the "doing" gifts.

PRAYER

DISCOVERY CENTERS

1. NAPKIN HOLDERS

DO: Before class, if you have younger students, make a full-size pattern with poster board using the pattern and instructions on page 61. (Older students may be able to make the shape using copies of page 61. Also, you might want to make more than one pattern, depending on your class size.) Distribute the patterns and the half sheets of poster board to the students. Ask the students to trace the patterns on their sheets of poster board. After they cut out the shape, ask the students to fold the poster board to form the napkin holder. (You may want to demonstrate using your pattern.) Ask students to work together to hold the sides in place as they tape them together. Then they may decorate the napkin holders with markers and stickers.

DISCUSS: Tell the students that the napkin holder is a reminder of the doing gifts. Ask: **Is kindness a "speaking" or "doing" gift? It could be either. How about leadership? It could be either.** Ask: **Why are we talking about kindness and leadership as "doing" gifts? In order to be a good leader, a person must do what she's leading others to do. Kindness is shown in deeds, not just words.** Ask: **Are any of the gifts better than others? Why or why not? Why would the gift of serving be a "doing" gift? If a person had the gift of giving, what could he give? How would a person with the gift of kindness act? Which gift do you think you might have?**

MATERIALS
a half sheet of poster board for each student, pencils, rulers, scissors, colored tape, markers, stickers, copies of the pattern on page 61 (for older students)

2. THE BROOM

DO: Practice this string figure before class so that you can guide your students as they learn it. Ask students to tie the two ends of their string together to form a large loop.

MATERIALS
one piece of string or yarn 2 yards long for each student

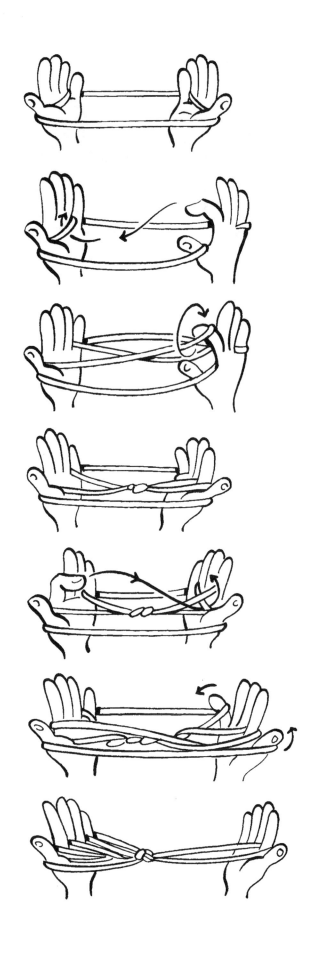

Position the loop so that it hangs around the thumbs, stretches across both palms, and loops around the small fingers.

The right pointer finger goes under the left palm string. Pull it out a bit.

Twist this new loop by rotating the pointer finger around, down and up. (The twist should now be in the string, not around the finger.)

Pull this twisted loop out as far as it will go.

The left pointer finger picks up the right palm string between the strings of the right pointer loop.

Drop the loops from the right thumb and right little finger.

Pull your right pointer finger out as far as it will go so that the loops move toward the left hand.

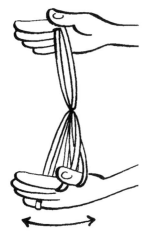

Move your right hand up and your left hand down. Swing the left hand back and forth to make this "broom" sweep.

DISCUSS: Say: **Who can you serve using a broom? Who serves you using a broom? If you don't have the gift of serving, does that mean that you can't help someone? If you don't have the gift of prophecy, does that mean you can't learn what God's will is? If you don't have the gift of giving, does that mean you don't have to give?**

Explain that we all serve and give and learn God's will. We are all to encourage each other and be kind. But for some of us, giving doesn't come naturally. Or serving doesn't come naturally. Or we have to work at encouraging others. The people who have these gifts find that these things just flow naturally from them. Their gifts are part of who they are. Ask: **What would be unfair about looking at someone else and saying, "She's not as good as I am, because she doesn't have the gift of teaching"?**

3. FOLD AND DRAW

DO: Remind the students about the faces they drew last week. Tell them that today they will draw bodies to go with the faces. Give each student two pieces of paper. They tape these, short sides together. Then they turn this strip vertically, and fold back half of the top piece. Now they unfold this and draw shoulders, collar, and upper arms above the fold. On the left side, they write "leading." On the right side, they write, "guide by example and words." Then they fold the top part back and pass the page to the student on their left.

MATERIALS

paper, tape, crayons or non-permanent markers, drawings of faces made last week

The next student folds the bottom page in half. Then tell them to unfold this and draw in the middle part. The taped line is the waist line. They draw arms and hands, shirt and pants or skirt. On the left side, they write, "giving." On the right side, they write, "kindness." Then they fold this back so that the bottom panel is face up. They pass the paper to the student on their left.

On this bottom panel, students draw legs and feet. On the left side they write, "serving." Then they pass the drawing to the student on their left who opens the entire drawing.

Put the face pictures drawn last week into a stack, face down. Each child draws a paper from the top of the stack. Then he tapes this head onto the body drawing he holds. You may display these in your room, or let students take them home.

DISCUSS: Ask: **What might a person with the gift of serving do? How could a person with the gift of giving help others? How might a person with the gift of kindness be a good steward? How could person who has the gift of leadership be a good steward?** Explain that we all give and help and try to be kind. Some of us have to work at it. But for others it comes naturally. They have that gift.

DISCOVERERS' DEBRIEFING

If you have time to review, gather as a large group and discuss your young discoverers' findings. Ask the following questions:

- **What is the most interesting thing you discovered today?**
- **What did you learn today that you did not know before?**
- **Are any of the gifts better than others? Explain.**
- **What might a person with the gift of serving do?**
- **How could a person with the gift of giving help others?**
- **How might a person with the gift of kindness be a good steward?**
- **How could person who has the gift of leadership be a good steward?**
- **How do these gifts help us be good stewards?**
- **If you don't have the gift of serving, does that mean you can't help someone? Explain.**

Review the Scripture for today.

Pray, thanking God for giving us these kinds of gifts. Ask God to show us what our gifts are, and to help us use these gifts to be good stewards and managers for him.

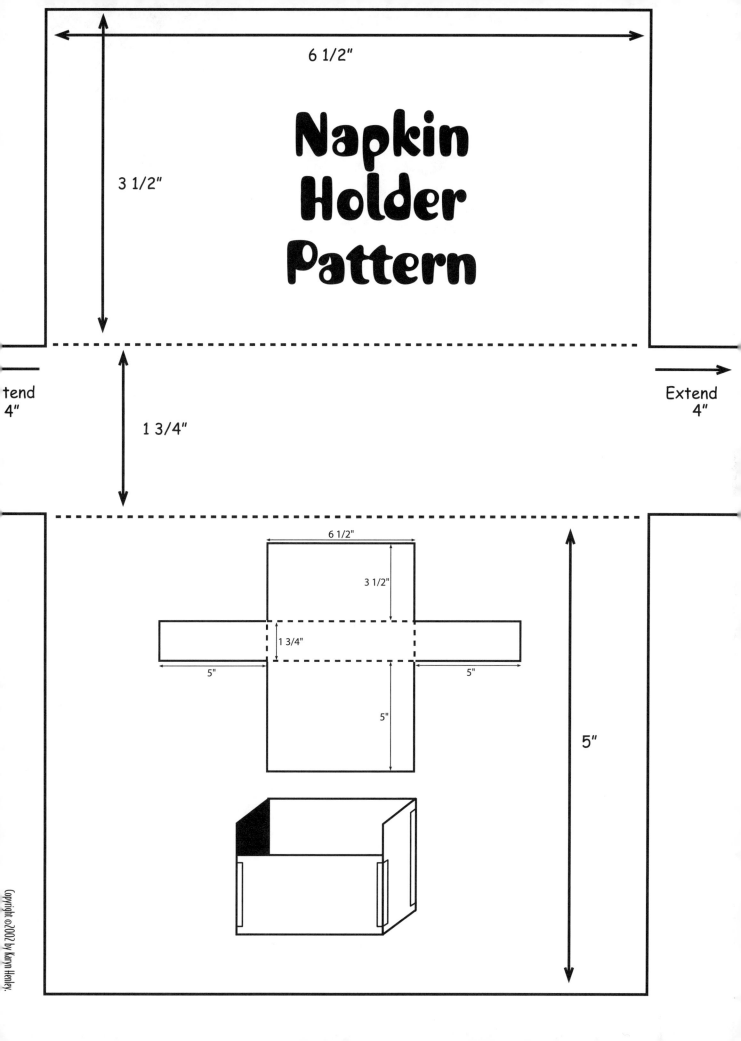

Napkin Holder Pattern

6 1/2"

3 1/2"

1 3/4"

tend 4"

Extend 4"

6 1/2"

3 1/2"

1 3/4"

5"

5"

5"

5"

Jesus Taught Us How to Serve

Scripture

"I have given you an example to follow. Do as I have done to you." John 13:15, NLT

Goal

Learn that we can look at Jesus to discover how to be a good servant.

INTRODUCTION

Bring as many small tools as you can: kitchen tools, garden spade, hammer, screwdriver and other building/repair tools, scissors, etc. As the students arrive, give each one a large piece of construction paper. Ask students to trace around as many tools as they can on their papers, even overlapping the outlines to make a design. Then they may color in the designs.

DISCOVERY RALLY

Gather the students together in a large group.

WHAT'S THE GOOD WORD?

Choose a student to read the Scripture for the day.

THE CHALLENGE

Ask the students to show their designs from the introductory activity. Ask them how some of these tools could be used to serve others. Then ask them to name the gifts discussed last week. Say: **It's easy to see how a person can be a servant if they have the gift of serving or giving or mercy or encouragement. But how can a leader be a servant? How can a teacher or prophet be a servant?**

Tell the students that today in their Discovery Centers they will learn about serving others by looking at a leader who was also a servant: Jesus.

PRAYER

DISCOVERY CENTERS

1. WHOSE MOM?

MATERIALS
pencils, copies of Whose Mom? (page 67), a Bible

DO: Give each student a pencil and a copy of the Whose Mom? page. Ask the students to draw a line from the clue to the name of the son. They may look up the Scriptures if they need help. When everyone has finished, read the clues and let them tell you the answers.

DISCUSS: Ask someone to read John 2:1-10. Ask: **How did Jesus serve his mother? How can you serve your parents?** Ask someone to read Mark 9:33-35. Ask: **How many people did Jesus tell his disciples to serve? He said they should be the "servant of all."** Say: **We are also Jesus' followers. He wants us, too, to be servants of all. Does this mean just the people of your**

church? Does it mean just the people of your neighborhood? Does it mean just the people of your race? Who does "all" leave out? How can you serve all people?

2. STEWARDS DOWN AND ACROSS

MATERIALS

pencils, Bibles, copies of Steward Acrostic (page 68)

DO: Work this acrostic together as a group. Ask students to look up each Scripture reference to discover the group that starts with the letter on that line. These are the kinds of people Jesus served. When they find the answers, they write the rest of that word beside the letter that begins the word. The answers are:

S ick
T roubled
E nemies
W idows
A fraid
R ich
D isciples

DISCUSS: Talk about each of the categories of people that students discovered in the acrostic. Ask: **How did Jesus serve the sick? He healed. How did he serve people who were troubled? He reminded them to trust in God. How did he serve his enemies? He loved them and lent to them. Widows? His heart went out to them. People who were afraid? He encouraged them. The rich? He loved them and told them how to have true treasure in heaven. His own disciples? He taught them. What can we learn about serving people by looking at Jesus?**

3. APRONS

MATERIALS

one inexpensive dish towel (or hand towel sized terrycloth fabric) for each child, pencils, rulers, scissors, fabric ribbon, a Bible

DO: Give each student a dish towel. Ask them to fold under the upper third of it. Then ask them to make a small mark close to the fold about 1"

from the left edge, a mark about 1" to the left of the center, a mark about 1" to the right of the center, and another small mark 1" from the right edge. Then they open the towel and cut a hole in it at each mark. Now they refold it and mark through the top holes onto the bottom layer of towel. They open it again and cut holes at each mark on this under side. They refold the towel. Give each student a 4' length of ribbon. Students thread the ribbon through both layers of the towel: up through the first hole, down through the second hole, up through the third hole, down through the fourth hole. Tell students to pull the ribbon through until there is an equal amount of ribbon extending from each side of the folded towel. This makes an apron.

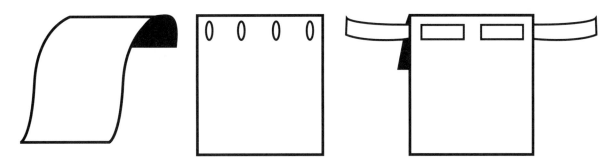

DISCUSS: Ask: **Why might a person wear an apron? Why do we sometimes get dirty when we are serving others?** Ask someone to read John 13:1-5 and 12-17. Ask: **Why did Jesus wrap a towel around his waist? Why did he wash his disciples' feet? What was he teaching his disciples? What can we learn from Jesus' example about serving others? How can you serve others this week?**

DISCOVERERS' DEBRIEFING

If you have time to review, gather as a large group and discuss your young discoverers' findings. Ask the following questions:

- **What is the most interesting thing you discovered today?**
- **What did you learn today that you did not know before?**
- **How many people did Jesus tell his disciples to serve?**
- **How can we be servants of all?**
- **Why did Jesus wrap a towel around his waist and wash his disciples' feet?**

- **What can we learn from Jesus' example about serving others?**
- **How can you serve others this week?**

Review the Scripture for today.

Pray, thanking God for Jesus' example as a servant. Ask God to help us be good servants, following Jesus' example.

NOTE: Make copies of the note to parents found on page 69. Send it home with the students today.

Also, during this next week, try to contact someone who represents a local, national, or overseas relief ministry. Ask if they would come and speak to one of your groups during your next class time. Suggestions:

- A person who works with your own church's food distribution program.
- A representative of Meals on Wheels.
- A Salvation Army representative.
- Someone who works with your city's food bank (Second Harvest, etc.)
- A Red Cross representative who helps distribute food for disaster relief.

Whose Mom?

Read the clues on the left. Draw a line from the clue to the son's name.

My mother was Jochebed. She made a basket boat to save me.

My mother prayed that God would give her a baby. I was the answer to her prayer. When I was still very young, she took me to the temple to live, so that I could serve God the rest of my life.

My mother laughed when God told her she would have a baby. I was born when she was 91 years old.

An angel told my mother that I would be born. My mother used a manger for my first cradle.

My mother was Eunice. She was a woman of faith. She taught me about God.

My mother was never a little girl.

My mother was married to King David.

My mother was Jesus' relative. She felt me jump inside her before I was born, and she was filled with the Holy Spirit.

Solomon
2 Samuel 12:24

Jesus
Luke 2:6, 7

Moses
Exodus 6:20

John the Baptist
Luke 1:41-44

Samuel
1 Samuel 1:20

Timothy
2 Timothy 1:5

Abel
Genesis 4:1, 2

Isaac
Genesis 18:13, 14

Steward Acrostic

S   Matthew 12:15

T   John 14:1, 27

E   Luke 6:35

W   Luke 7:12, 13

A   Matthew 10:29-31

R   Mark 10:17-22

D   Matthew 11:1

FROM YOUR CHILD'S TEACHER

Dear Parent,

As you may know, we are involved in a series of lessons concerning stewardship and servanthood. It is our goal to help each student understand what a steward is, and to understand that God intends for us to be good stewards over all he has given us.

We are also learning how to serve others. In order to make our learning practical, our class will be donating items to the poor and needy over the next few weeks. For this we need your help. We are asking that each student bring at least one item of canned or boxed non-perishable food next week. This will allow your child to be actively involved in putting into practice what we are learning: "When you did it to one of the least of these my brothers and sisters, you were doing it to me!" (Matthew 25:40).

It is a pleasure to be able to teach your child about stewardship and servanthood. Thank you for helping us accomplish that task. Feel free to call with any questions.

Teacher_____

Phone_____

Serving Those Who Hunger and Thirst

Scripture

"For I was hungry, and you fed me. I was thirsty, and you gave me a drink... when you did it to one of the least of these my brothers and sisters, you were doing it to me!" Matthew 25:35, 40

Goal

Learn that when we serve the hungry and thirsty, we serve the Lord.

INTRODUCTION

As students arrive, ask them to place the food items they brought in a large box or other collection area. Then give one student a small can of food. Everyone else closes their eyes. The student with the food hides it in a place that's not obvious, but where it can still be partially seen. This student tells everyone else when they can look. The students now look for the food with their eyes only, not saying anything or touching anything. When a student sees the food, she says, "Lunch!" and then sits down quietly. One by one, the students see the hidden food and sit down. When all students have discovered the food, ask the first one who saw it to hide it for another round of the game.

DISCOVERY RALLY

Gather the students together in a large group.

WHAT'S THE GOOD WORD?

Choose a student to read the Scripture for the day.

THE CHALLENGE

Ask the students to tell you what their favorite food is. Ask them what they had for breakfast. Ask them when they expect to have their next meal. Ask what it feels like to be hungry. Then say: **In 1998, 10.5 million families in the United States did not have enough food to meet their basic needs. About 4 million American children under the age of 12 go hungry every day.** Tell the students that the food they brought today will help needy people who might not otherwise get to eat.

Tell the students that in their Discovery Centers today, they will find out more about helping the hungry.

PRAYER

DISCOVERY CENTERS

1. FEEDING THE HUNGRY

DO: If you have a guest speaker, introduce this person to your students. Ask the speaker to tell your students how he or she helps the hungry. You may want this person to tell how people can get involved in helping this ministry. Allow the students to ask questions. If they can't think of questions, you might ask them to think of a "why" question, then a "what" question, then a "how" question. Other questions might start with "when," "who," or "what if."

If you don't have a guest speaker, spread newspaper across the work surface.

MATERIALS

If you were not able to get a guest, you will need: plastic shelf liner in a solid color, four different colors of acrylic paint, four paper plates, paper towels, permanent markers, an apple cut in half, a carrot cut in half lengthwise, an ear of corn, a stalk of celery, a potato cut in half lengthwise, a bell pepper cut in half, and newspaper

Give each student a 14" length of shelf liner to make a placemat. Ask students to write on the mat, "'When you did it to one of these, you were doing it to me.' Matthew 25:40." Spread each paper plate with a different color of acrylic paint. Set out the vegetables. Tell the students to make vegetable prints on their placemats by pressing the vegetables onto the paint on the plates, then pressing them onto the placemats. Set them aside to dry.

DISCUSS: Ask: **Have you ever been hungry? How do you know when you're really hungry? What do you do when you're hungry? What might it be like if you couldn't find food?** Say: **Feeding the hungry is one way to be a good steward and servant in God's Kingdom. Why? Why did Jesus say that when we feed the hungry, we're feeding him? Who are some people who might need food? How can we help them?**

2. HOMEMADE CUPS

MATERIALS
plain paper, scissors, pencils, a pitcher or jug of water, a Bible

DO: Give each student a piece of paper. Ask students to fold the paper so that one corner becomes a point as shown. Then they cut off the excess paper and turn the folded triangle so that the fold is at the bottom. Now with a pencil, they make a dot at about the center of the right edge of the triangle. They fold the left bottom corner up to meet the dot on the right side. Then they fold the right bottom corner to the left side in the same way. Next they fold the top front flap down. They turn the paper over and flip the other top flap down. Then they gently squeeze the cup so the mouth of it opens. Pour a bit of water in each student's cup so they can have a drink.

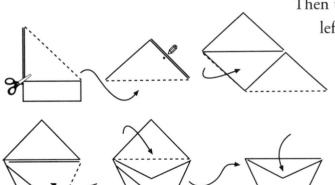

DISCUSS: Ask: **When do you get most thirsty? What does it feel like to be thirsty? What do you do when you're thirsty? What might it be like if you couldn't find any-**

thing to drink? Say: **Giving the thirsty a drink is one way to be a good steward and servant in God's Kingdom. Why?** Ask someone to read Matthew 10:42. Ask: **Who are the "little ones?"** These could be children, or they could be people whom others would consider unimportant or unworthy of being helped. Ask: **What do you think the "reward" is? Why did Jesus say that when we give water to someone who's thirsty, we're helping him? Who are some people who might need water? How can we help them?**

3. SCROLL ROLL

MATERIALS
a Bible, paper, pen, rubber bands, an audio tape or CD player and tape or CD of your choice

DO: Before class, copy the following Scripture references onto paper, one Scripture reference per piece of paper: Exodus 16:2, 3, 13-15; Judges 15:16-19; Ruth 2:1-3; 1 Kings 17:1-6; 1 Kings 17:7-16; Psalm 107:8, 9; Psalm 146:5-7; Proverbs 22:9; Proverbs 25:21; Isaiah 58:6, 7; 14-16; Luke 16:19-25; John 6:5-13. Roll up each piece of paper, and place a rubber band around each one.

Ask students to line up in a circle, front to back. Give one student one of the scrolls. Students are to pass this scroll around the circle: The first student passes it overhead to the student behind her. He rolls it on the ground between his feet to the student behind him. This student passes it overhead, the next rolls it between his feet, and so on, over and under. Students begin passing the scroll when you begin the music. They stop when you stop the music. The student who holds the scroll (or to whom it is being rolled when the music stops) opens the scroll and looks up the Scripture reference written on it. This student reads the Scripture aloud from the Bible. Then give that student a new scroll, and start the music again for a second round.

DISCUSS: After the game has gone on for awhile, ask everyone to sit down for a discussion. Ask: **What do these verses say about people who are hungry or thirsty?** Or ask: **Why were these people hungry or thirsty? How did they get food or drink? Why is God interested in feeding people? Why does God want us to take care of hungry people? What did Jesus mean when he said, "When you do it to one of these, you do it to me"? Who are the hungry and thirsty people who need our help? What can we do about it?**

DISCOVERERS' DEBRIEFING

Discoverers' Debriefing Debriefing

If you have time to review, gather as a large group and discuss your young discoverers' findings. Ask the following questions:

- **What is the most interesting thing you discovered today?**
- **What did you learn today that you did not know before?**
- **Why is caring for the hungry and thirsty important to God?**
- **How is caring for the hungry and thirsty a way to be a good steward and servant in God's Kingdom?**
- **Why did Jesus say that when we give food to hungry people, we're feeding him?**
- **How can we feed the hungry and give water to the thirsty?**

Review the Scripture for today.

Pray, thanking God for providing food and water for us. Ask him to give us the heart of a servant and show us how to help those who are hungry and thirsty.

NOTE: Make copies of the note to parents found at the end of this session plan. Send it home with the students today.

Also, during this next week, try to contact someone who represents a local, national, or overseas ministry that serves prisoners or strangers (even children you don't know and others overseas are strangers), ask if they would come and speak to one of your groups during your next class time. Suggestions:

1) A person who works with your own church in prison ministry or in community service.
2) A representative of Samaritan's Purse.
3) A Salvation Army representative.
4) Someone who works in your city in a school attended by needy children.
5) A Red Cross representative who works with disaster relief.
6) Someone who works with Compassion International.

*Statistics in the Challenge portion of this lesson come from the Food Research and Action Center, www.frac.org.

FROM YOUR CHILD'S TEACHER

Dear Parent,

As you know, we are involved in a series of lessons concerning stewardship and servanthood. It is our goal to help each student understand what a steward is, and to understand that God intends for us to be good stewards over all he has given us. We are also learning how to serve others. Thank you for your help in this.

This week, in order to make our learning practical, our class will be donating school supplies for the poor and needy. So we ask for your help once again. We are asking that each student bring at least one item of school supplies for a school that serves the needy. This will allow your child to be actively involved in putting into practice what we are learning: "When you did it to one of the least of these my brothers and sisters, you were doing it to me!" (Matthew 25:40).

It is a pleasure to be able to teach your child about stewardship and servanthood. Thank you for helping us accomplish that task. Feel free to call with any questions.

Teacher_____

Phone_____

Serving Prisoners and Strangers

Scripture

"I was a stranger, and you invited me into your home... I was in prison, and you visited me...when you did it to one of the least of these my brothers and sisters, you were doing it to me!" Matthew 25:35, 36, 40, NLT

Goal

Learn that when we serve prisoners and strangers, we serve the Lord.

INTRODUCTION

Have markers and crayons available. As students arrive, give each student a paper lunch bag. Tell them to make a colorful design on the bag. Then they can put the school supplies they brought into the bag. Give these to a school that serves needy children.

DISCOVERY RALLY

Discovery Rally
y Rally
Discovery Rally

Gather the students together in a large group.

WHAT'S THE GOOD WORD?

Choose a student to read the Scripture for the day.

THE CHALLENGE

Ask the children what they think of when they hear the word "stranger." Say: **We've been taught to stay away from strangers. There are some strangers who would be dangerous, and we must be careful. But the word "stranger" simply means someone we don't know. If a friend needs help, we are usually quick to help out. But if someone we don't know needs help, it's not so easy. In fact, it's easy to ignore someone we don't know. How do we know who to help?**

Tell the students that in their Discovery Centers today they will find out about strangers and how to help them.

PRAYER

DISCOVERY CENTERS

Discovery Centers
y Centers

1. MAGAZINE HELP-A-STRANGER HUNT

MATERIALS
six copies of the Help-a-Stranger List (page 82), two magazines that contain pictures of the items on this list, pencils

DO: Before class, go through the magazines to remove any inappropriate pictures or articles. Divide your group into two teams. Give each team a pencil and the list. Each team should choose a Record-Keeper who will use the pencil and list to keep track of the items they find. Now give each team a magazine. When you say, "Begin," they have ten minutes to find each item on their list in the magazine. (You may adjust the time to fit the needs of your class schedule.) When they find an item on their list, the Record-Keeper writes down the magazine page number where they found it. The team to find all the items first wins.

DISCUSS: Say: **The items you were looking for are items that can be shared. It's easy to share them with friends. It's not so easy to share them with strangers. How do you know which strangers to help? If you're not sure, ask your parents, a teacher, or another adult you trust.** Encourage your group to list strangers they can help, and tell how they can help them. Some examples may include:

1) A new person at school (they can welcome the new student and help her find her way around)
2) An older person going into a building (they can hold the door open for this person)
3) A new family who moves into a house in their neighborhood (they can visit along with their parents)
4) People in foreign countries (they can give to missions, pray for these nations, and even go on missions trips)
5) People who have experienced a disaster, such as an earthquake or hurricane (they can give food, clothes, and money to relief workers)
6) A church group or choir visiting from another town (they can offer their houses as a places to stay)

Also suggest that one way to help prisoners and strangers is to give food, clothing, money, and supplies to people and groups who work with prisoners and strangers. And we can volunteer our time to help these groups. That way, people who are experienced and wise about working with strangers can supervise us and show us the best way to help. Ask if any of the children or their families have helped strangers or prisoners. If so, ask them to tell about that experience.

2. ENCOURAGEMENT SCRIPTURE CARDS

MATERIALS
If you were not able to get a guest, you will need: colored index cards, envelopes, Bibles, markers or pens

DO: If you have a guest speaker, introduce this person to your students. Ask the speaker to tell your students how he or she helps prisoners or strangers. You may want this person to tell how people can get involved in helping with such a ministry. Allow the students to ask questions. If they can't think of questions, you might ask them to think of a "why" question, then a "what" question, then a "how" question. Other questions might start with "when," "who," or "what if."

If you don't have a guest speaker, give each student an index card, envelope, Bible, and pen or marker. Give each student a Scripture reference to look up. See the list below. Each student writes his Scripture on his card. Students may also draw designs on their cards. Then they place them in the envelopes so the cards can be given to a prison ministry group or someone who works with people your students don't know.

Psalm 55:22   Philippians 4:6
Psalm 145:8   1 Peter 5:7
Matthew 11:28   2 Corinthians 12:9
Romans 15:13   Psalm 91:1
John 16:33   Hebrews 4:16
James 4:8   Psalm 23:1, 2
Psalm 121:1, 2

DISCUSS: Ask the students to read aloud the encouragement Scriptures on their cards. After each Scripture is read, ask: **Why might this Scripture be encouraging to a prisoner or someone who is a stranger to you? Why is God interested in prisoners? Why is God interested in strangers? How are we serving Jesus by serving prisoners and strangers?** Ask someone to read Luke 24:13-16 and 28-32. Say: **These two men thought Jesus was a stranger. When they were kind to the stranger, they were really being kind to Jesus! Who are some strangers we might serve, and how might we serve them?** See the discussion in center #1 for some guidance in answering these questions.

3. PRAYERS AND ANGELS

Before class, contact a retirement home or nursing home, and get the names of people for whom students can make these angels. Write each person's name on an index card. Another option is to use names of senior citizens in

MATERIALS

index cards, pencils or pens, 12" wide aluminum foil, chenille wires, one egg carton for every 12 students (polystyrene foam cartons work best), ruler, scissors, permanent markers, a Bible

your church who may be confined to home. Or if your guest today works with prisoners or strangers, you may want to give the angels to them to distribute among the people they work with.

DO: Give each student two 6" wide pieces of foil. They cut one of these in half, making two 6" x 6" pieces. These are the angel wings. The larger piece is the body. Students fold all the pieces accordion-style as shown below. Cut the lid off the egg carton. Then cut the individual cups apart. Give one cup to each student. Students gently slip a chenille wire through one side of the cup and out the opposite side about two inches. This is twisted into a loop. Lay the other end of the chenille wire under a center fold of the body so that the bottom of the cup is up, making the face of the angel. Set a wing on each side of the body. Wrap a second chenille wire around the wings, body, and first wire, close to the head. Gently fold out the foil wings and body. Draw a face on the bottom of the cup.

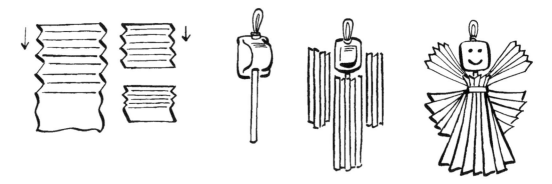

Give each student an index card. Ask them to write on it: "An angel to remind you that someone's praying for you." Then as a group, pray for the people whose names are on the cards. If you have no names, pray for the general group of people that these angels will go to. During the coming week, deliver these angels and cards to your chosen recipients.

DISCUSS: Ask someone to read Hebrews 13:1-3. If you have time, read Genesis 18:1-10, 22, and 19:1. Talk about who these "strangers" were and what Abraham did for them. Ask: **Who are strangers? How can we help strangers?** See the discussion in center #1 to guide your conversation. Say: **We can always help by praying for them. If it might be dangerous to help a stranger, or if we don't know how to help, we can still pray for them.**

DISCOVERERS' DEBRIEFING

If you have time to review, gather as a large group and discuss your young discoverers' findings. Ask the following questions:

- **What is the most interesting thing you discovered today?**
- **What did you learn today that you did not know before?**
- **How do you know which strangers to help?**
- **Who are strangers? How can we help them?**
- **Why is God interested in prisoners?**
- **Why is God interested in strangers?**
- **How are we serving Jesus by serving prisoners and strangers?**

Review the Scripture for today.

Pray, thanking God for his love of all people, even prisoners and strangers. Ask God to bless them, and to help us be wise in knowing how to serve prisoners and strangers.

NOTE: Make copies of the note to parents found on page 83. Send it home with the students today.

Also, during this next week, try to contact someone who represents a local, national, or overseas ministry that serves people who need clothing or shelter. Ask if they would come and speak to one of your groups during your next class time. Suggestions:

- A person who works with your own church in providing clothing or housing for the needy.
- A representative of Habitat for Humanity.
- A Salvation Army representative.
- Someone who works in your city with the mentally and physically disabled.
- A Red Cross representative who works with disaster relief.

Help-a-Stranger List

1) a house _____

2) food _____

3) a smile _____

4) school supplies: books or pens or pencils, etc. _____

5) drinks (water, juice, or soda) _____

6) money _____

7) a door to welcome someone _____

8) packages to carry for someone _____

9) clothes _____

10) toys _____

11) a helping hand _____

12) toothbrush, toothpaste, or soap _____

FROM YOUR CHILD'S TEACHER

Dear Parent,

As you know, we are involved in a series of lessons concerning stewardship and servanthood. It is our goal to help each student understand what a steward is, and to understand that God intends for us to be good stewards over all he has given us. We are also learning how to serve others.

Next week, we will be learning about serving those who need clothes or housing. In order to make our learning practical, our class will be donating clothing for the poor and needy. For this we need your help. We are asking that each student bring at least one item of clothing in good condition next week. This will allow your child to be actively involved in putting into practice what we are learning: "When you did it to one of the least of these my brothers and sisters, you were doing it to me!" (Matthew 25:40).

It is a pleasure to be able to teach your child about stewardship. Thank you for helping us accomplish that task. Feel free to call with any questions.

Teacher_____

Phone_____

Serving the Needy

Scripture

"I was naked, and you gave me clothing...when you did it to one of the least of these my brothers and sisters, you were doing it to me!" Matthew 25:36, 40, NLT

Goal

Learn that when we clothe and shelter the needy, we serve the Lord.

INTRODUCTION

Bring a large box or two to hold the clothing items that the students bring. As students arrive, ask them to put their clothing donations into the boxes. Then give each student a piece of plain paper and a crayon. Students place the paper across the sole of one of their shoes, and then rub over the paper with a crayon to reveal the pattern of the sole on the paper. This can be done with shoes on or off, according to the wishes of each student. When the student has finished making the pattern of his shoe, he gives you the piece of paper. After you've gathered a few of these "sole rubbings," mix them up and give them to the students. The students then try to discover whose shoe matches the pattern of the paper they have. To keep the game going, when they find the owner of the shoe pattern, they can give the paper back to you and get another one.

DISCOVERY RALLY

Gather the students together in a large group.

WHAT'S THE GOOD WORD?

Choose a student to read the Scripture for the day.

THE CHALLENGE

Ask the students to raise their hands if they have more than one pair of shoes. Say: **People who own more than one pair of shoes are rich by the world's standards. Most people in the world have only one pair of shoes, and many don't have any shoes at all. Poor people can't get many of the things they need, like enough food, clothes, and medical care. Some don't even have houses.** Ask: **How would you feel if you didn't have enough clothes, food, or housing?** Say: **Many poor people feel helpless and hopeless. They may feel angry. They may be focused on their worries more than anything else. Many children who grow up poor don't know how to be anything else.** Tell students that in their Discovery Centers today, they will find out about being a good steward by serving those who need clothes and shelter.

PRAYER

DISCOVERY CENTERS

1. PASS OR PAIR

DO: Before class, make two copies of each of the two pages of Pass or Pair Scriptures. Cut the Scriptures apart so they can be used as game cards. There should be two of each Scripture. Mix the Scripture cards up and deal them to the students. It doesn't matter if a few students get one card more than the others; deal out all the cards. Students look at their cards and try to make a match. Choose one student to go first. He places any matching pairs on the table in front of him, reading aloud the Scripture from each pair. Then the person on his left places

> **MATERIALS**
> two copies each of the two pages of Pass or Pair Scriptures (pages 89, 90)

down any pairs, reading the Scriptures. If someone doesn't have a match, they say, "Pass." When all students have had a chance to pair or pass, ask each student to choose one card from their hand and pass it to the person on their left. Now go around the group again, pairing or passing with the newly received cards. Continue in this way until all the cards have been paired and read.

DISCUSS: Ask: **What did you discover from these Scriptures about God's attitude toward the poor? What did you discover about how we can be God's stewards? Why do you think God is so concerned about the poor?**

2. BRAIDED BELTS

MATERIALS

a variety of colors of fabric ribbon 1" wide (6 yards of ribbon for each student), scissors, a Bible

DO: Each student should work with a partner. Cut three two-yard lengths of ribbon for each student. Students lay the three strips on top of each other and tie them into a knot at one end. One student holds the knotted end of her partner's ribbons while her partner braids them: Separate the three ribbons close to the knotted end. Bring the right ribbon over the center ribbon. (It now becomes the center ribbon.) Bring the left

ribbon over the center ribbon. (It now becomes the center ribbon.) Pull all of this until it is firm, but not too tight. Students keep braiding right over center, left over center, right over center, left over center, until they reach the end of the ribbons. They tie this end into a knot. Then the partners change places so the second belt can be braided. Students place these belts into the box of clothing that will be given to the needy.

DISCUSS: Tell the students the true story of another student whose school was collecting clothing for the needy. This student went through her old clothes to find things to give away. Then she began to think about what it must feel like to be poor and always have to wear something old that someone else didn't want to wear anymore. So she went to her closet. She took out her newest dress, which she liked very much, and she gave it away. Ask: **Why is it easy to give away something that is**

worn out and old or out of fashion? Ask someone to read Luke 6:31. Ask:
**How can this apply to helping the poor? If you were poor, how would you
want others to treat you? How do we serve Jesus by serving the poor?**

3. ANGEL SHIRTS

MATERIALS

If you were not able to get a guest, you will
need: fabric paint, fabric markers, old
newspapers, paper plates or disposable pie
tins (one for each color of paint), paper towels,
and T-shirts of various sizes (not necessarily
sized to fit your students)

DO: If you have a guest speaker, introduce this person to
your students. Ask the speaker to tell your students how
she helps those who need clothes or housing. You may
want to tell how people can get involved with such a
ministry. Allow the students to ask questions. You might
ask them to think of a "why" question, then a "what" question, then a "how" question. Other questions might start with "when," "who,"
or "what if."

If you don't have a guest speaker, give each student a T-shirt and several sheets
of newspaper. Students fold the newspaper into a thick padding and stick it
inside the T-shirt between the front and back. Students use the fabric markers
to draw on the front of the shirt. They draw a
circle and then a triangle under it as shown
below. This becomes the head and body of the
angel. Fill the bottom of each paper plate or
pie tin with fabric paint. Students press their
hands into the fabric paint, then onto the
front of the T-shirt to make angel wings as
shown. Students wipe their hands with paper
towels and then wash them. Let the T-shirts
dry. Then add them to the collection of clothing you will give to the needy.

DISCUSS: Ask someone to read Acts 10:1-4. Ask: **Why did God choose to
honor Cornelius? Why is it important to God that we give to the poor?** Say:
**God loves the poor and wants them to have what they need. When we give
to the poor, we reflect the character of God, because he is generous, loving,
and kind. Seeing the needs of others and helping them creates in us**

humble, thankful hearts. It allows us to see how blessed we truly are, and to share that blessing with others. Ask someone to read James 2:2-5. Ask: **What is this Scripture talking about? What is the attitude that God wants us to have toward the poor? How do we serve Jesus when we serve the poor?**

DISCOVERERS' DEBRIEFING

If you have time to review, gather as a large group and discuss your young discoverers' findings. Ask the following questions:
- **What is the most interesting thing you discovered today?**
- **What did you learn today that you did not know before?**
- **What is God's attitude toward the poor?**
- **How can we be God's stewards helping the poor?**
- **How can the "Golden Rule" apply to helping the poor?**
- **How do we serve Jesus by serving the poor?**

Review the Scripture for today.

Pray, thanking God for our clothes and houses. Ask God to guide us as we learn how to serve the poor and needy.

NOTE: During this next week, try to contact a doctor, nurse, or home health-care professional and ask if they would come and speak to one of your groups during your next class time. Suggestions:
- A person from your own church who is a health care provider.
- Someone who works at or directs a nursing home.
- Someone who works in your city with the mentally and physically disabled.
- A Red Cross representative who helps people who are hurt or sick.
- Someone in medical missions.

Pass or Pair Scriptures

"If there are any poor people in your towns...do not be hard-hearted or tight-fisted toward them. Instead, be generous and lend them whatever they need." Deuteronomy 15:7, 8	"There will always be some among you who are poor. That is why I am commanding you to share your resources freely with the poor." Deuteronomy 15:11
"Never take advantage of poor laborers....Pay them their wages each day before sunset because they are poor and are counting on it." Deuteronomy 24:14	"Give fair judgment to the poor and the orphan; uphold the rights of the oppressed and the destitute." Psalm 82:3
"Those who oppress the poor insult their Maker, but those who help the poor honor him." Proverbs 14:31	"It is sin to despise one's neighbors; blessed are those who help the poor." Proverbs 14:21
"Those who mock the poor insult their Maker; those who rejoice at the misfortune of others will be punished." Proverbs 17:5	"If you help the poor, you are lending to the Lord—and he will repay you!" Proverbs 19:17
"Those who shut their ears to the cries of the poor will be ignored in their own time of need." Proverbs 21:13	"Blessed are those who are generous, because they feed the poor." Proverbs 22:9

"Whoever gives to the poor will lack nothing. But a curse will come upon those who close their eyes to poverty." Proverbs 28:27	"The godly know the rights of the poor; the wicked don't care to know." Proverbs 29:7
"Speak up for the poor and helpless, and see that they get justice." Proverbs 31:9	The king "'made sure that justice and and help were given to the poor and needy.... Isn't that what it means to know me?' asks the Lord." Jeremiah 22:16
"Who can find a virtuous and capable wife?... She extends a helping hand to the poor and opens her arms to the needy." Proverbs 31:10, 20	"To the poor, O Lord, you are a refuge from the storm. To the needy in distress you are a shelter from the rain and the heat." Isaiah 25:4
"I want you to share your food with the hungry and to welcome poor wanderers into your homes. Give clothes to those who need them." Isaiah 58:7	"Sodom's sins were pride, laziness, and gluttony, while the poor and needy suffered outside her door." Ezekiel 16:49
"Sell what you have and give to those in need. This will store up treasure for you in heaven!" Luke 12:33	"When you put on a luncheon or a dinner,...invite the poor, the crippled, the lame, and the blind." Luke 14:13

Serving the Sick

Scripture

"I was sick, and you cared for me...when you did it to one of the least of these my brothers and sisters, you were doing it to me!"   *Matthew 25:36, 40, NLT*

Goal

Learn that when we serve the sick, we serve the Lord.

INTRODUCTION

As students arrive, give each of them three pieces of lined notebook paper and a pencil. Ask them to write the alphabet down the left side, skipping two lines between each letter. Then they go back down the alphabet and try to think of a feeling that starts with each letter. They write the name of the feeling. Beside it they draw a face that shows that feeling. For X, they can use a word starting with "ex." If they get stuck, they can go to the next letter. They can also ask classmates for suggestions.

DISCOVERY RALLY

Gather the students together in a large group.

WHAT'S THE GOOD WORD?

Choose a student to read the Scripture for the day.

THE CHALLENGE

Ask students to tell you some of the feelings they listed for each letter. Then say: **All our different feelings or emotions are one thing that makes us different from animals. Sometimes our feelings are connected to whether our bodies are well or sick. God has made our bodies to be the most amazing of all his creations.** Ask the students to make a fist. Say: **Your heart is about the size of your fist.** Now ask them to place a hand on their heart. Say: **Your heart circulates your blood through your entire body over 1,000 times every day.** Ask the students to look at the blood vessels that show on the inside of their arms close to their wrists. Say: **If your blood vessels were laid out end to end, they would go about 60,000 miles! Most of the time, your amazing body stays healthy. But sometimes it gets sick or hurt. You may get a fever, which is your body's way of trying to kill off a virus or bacteria. When some people get sick, they enjoy having people call or visit them. Other people want to be left alone so they can rest.**

Tell the students that in their Discovery Centers today, they will find out about serving people who are sick.

PRAYER

DISCOVERY CENTERS

1. HANKY BOUQUETS

NOTE: Before class, get the names of three sick people or elderly people who are home bound.

MATERIALS
one handkerchief for each student, green chenille wires or floral wire, fabric ribbon, scissors

Your groups will make a bouquet for each of these three people. Then during the coming week, take or send the bouquets to each person. It will be even better if your students can take the bouquets to these people.

DO: Practice making a hanky flower before class so that you can help the students as needed. Give each student a handkerchief. Ask them to fold it in half from corner to corner as shown below. Then the right and left points are folded to the center. The bottom point is folded up. Insert the wire as shown. Students may be able to punch the wire through the fabric, or they can cut a tiny slit with scissors for the wire to slip through. Sides are again brought to the center, covering the hole where the wire is inserted. Pinch all the layers closed as shown and tie snugly with fabric ribbon. When students are finished, gather all their flowers and tie them into a bouquet with more ribbon. Tell them who these flowers will go to, and pray for that person.

DISCUSS: Ask the students if they know anyone who is sick. Pray as a group for anyone they name. Then ask: **How can we care for the sick?** Say: **One of the most important things is to help sick people feel comfortable. How could you do this? What could you do for a sick person to help keep them occupied if they have to stay in bed? What kinds of things could you say to cheer up a sick person? How is caring for a sick person a way to care for Jesus?**

2. BEDSIDE MANNERS BINGO

DO: Give each student a pencil and a Bingo card. Call out items at random from the Bedside Manners List, placing a mark beside each one you've called so you won't repeat it. If a student has that item on his bingo page, she crosses it out. The first student to cross out an entire row across, down, or diagonally wins. If you have an early winner, you may want to hand your list to the winner and let the winner continue to call out items from the list until you have a second winner.

MATERIALS

enough copies of the Bedside Manners Bingo page (page 96) so that each child gets a card, pencils, a copy of the Bedside Manners List for yourself: read to them; spend time with them; help with homework; run errands; take them snacks; give them games; send flowers; give them books; clean their room; give them puzzles; send cards; get them a pillow; get their mail; pray for them; give them good videos; give them a radio

DISCUSS: Now talk about the items. Ask: **Which of these would help a sick person feel more comfortable? Which would help to keep them occupied if they have to stay still? Why might cleaning their room help them? Why might it be important to help them with homework? How does sending a card help a sick person? Do you have other suggestions that would help sick people? Why is God interested in sick people? What did Jesus mean when he said, "When you care for the sick, you care for me"?**

3. THE THUMBLESS GROUP

DO: If you have a guest speaker, introduce this person to your students. Ask the speaker to tell your students how he or she helps the sick. You may want this person to tell how people can get involved in helping with such a ministry. Allow the students to ask questions. If they can't think of ques-

MATERIALS

If you were able to get a guest who works wi sick people, students can visit with that pers in this center today. If you were not able to g guest, you will need: first aid adhesive tape, small ball to toss and catch, paper and crayon

tions, you might ask them to think of a "why" question, then a "what" question, then a "how" question. Other questions might start with "when," "who," or "what if."

If you don't have a guest speaker, tape each student's thumbs to the palms of his hands. Then play a Scripture memory ball toss. Ask a student to read the Scripture for the day. Then this student tosses the ball to another student. When this student catches the ball, she says the verse and then tosses it to another student. This student says the verse and tosses it on. Continue in this way until everyone has had a chance to say the verse. Then ask the students to sit at a table. Give everyone a piece of paper. Let them get their own crayon. Ask them to write the verse on the paper. All of this will be done with difficulty, of course, since their thumbs will be useless. The point is to feel the frustration that sick and injured people feel when they have a hard time doing things that are normally easy to do.

DISCUSS: Ask: **What feelings did you have in this group today? Why? Why do sick and injured people often feel frustrated? How can we encourage them?** Say: **It's important to let sick and injured people do as much as they possibly can for themselves. Why? Why are we serving Jesus when we serve the sick?**

DISCOVERERS' DEBRIEFING

If you have time to review, gather as a large group and discuss your young discoverers' findings. Ask the following questions:
- **What is the most interesting thing you discovered today?**
- **What did you learn today that you did not know before?**
- **How can we care for the sick?**
- **Why is God interested in sick people?**
- **Why do sick and injured people often feel frustrated? How can we encourage them?**
- **What did Jesus mean when he said, "When you care for the sick, you care for me"?**

Review the Scripture for today.

Pray, thanking God for being our Creator, our Healer, and our Helper. Ask him to heal the sick. Ask God to show us how to care for the sick and serve them.

Bedside Manners Bingo

Clean their room	Pray for them	Help with homework
Send flowers	Run errands	Send cards to them
Give them a radio	Give them good videos	Give them books

Pray for them	Help with homework	Get their mail
Run errands	Send cards to them	Get them a pillow
Give them good videos	Give them books	Give them puzzles

Help with homework	Get their mail	Run errands
Send cards to them	Give them a radio	Give them good videos
Give them books	Give them puzzles	Give them games

Get their mail	Run errands	Send cards to them
Send flowers	Give them good videos	Give them books
Give them puzzles	Give them games	Spend time with them

Run errands	Send cards to them	Give them a radio
Send flowers	Give them books	Give them puzzles
Give them games	Spend time with them	Read to them

Send cards to them	Give them a radio	Give them good videos
Give them books	Give them puzzles	Get them a pillow
Spend time with them	Read to them	Take them snacks